ZEN NO SHO

ZEN NO SHO

The Calligraphy of
Fukushima Keidō Rōshi

Edited by Jason M. Wirth

Preface by George Hisaeda, Consul General of Japan, Atlanta
Foreword by Lloyd Nick, Director, Oglethorpe University Museum of Art

Contributions from
Audrey Yoshiko Seo, Stephen Addiss,
Stephen J. Goldberg, Ronald L. Carlisle

CLEAR LIGHT PUBLISHERS
Santa Fe, New Mexico

Dedicated to

Fukushima Keidō Rōshi

In Homage, Gratitude,
and Friendship.

CLEAR LIGHT PUBLISHERS

823 Don Diego, Santa Fe, New Mexico 87505
www.clearlightbooks.com

First Edition
10 9 8 7 6 5 4 3 2 1

Library of Congress Cataloging-in-Publication Data

Zen no sho : the calligraphy of Fukushima Keidō Rōshi / edited by Jason
M. Wirth ; preface by George Hisaeda ; foreword by Lloyd Nick.-- 1st ed.
    p. cm.
 1. Fukushima, Keidō, 1933---Criticism and interpretation. 2.
Calligraphy, Zen. I. Wirth, Jason M., 1963- II. Title.
  ND1457.B836F8539 2003
  745.6'19956--dc21

                                              2002156509

  ISBN: 1-57416-070-2
  ISBN: 1-57416-071-0

Cover image: *Zen*, ink on paper, 11" x 10.25".

禪

Book design and typography by Carol O'Shea.
Printed in the U.S.A.

Zen No Sho: The Calligraphy of Fukushima Keidō Rōshi
Oglethorpe University Museum of Art, Atlanta, Georgia
February 25–May 11, 2003, first venue of national tour

Table of Contents

Acknowledgments

We would like to thank here the many people without whom this book and exhibition would not have been possible.

For their generous help with the promotion and support of the exhibit, we would like to thank Roger Kintzel and Booker T. Izell and the *Atlanta Journal-Constitution*, Tom Bigelow and bigelow & eigel, inc., Rodger French and the DeKalb Council for the Arts, Audrey Monks and Swissôtel Atlanta. For their outstanding help with the scanning and production of the images, we would like to thank Ray Epperson, B. J. Morton, and Bill Morton of Setscan.com.

For their enthusiastic, generous and unqualified support, we would like to thank the Office of the Consul General of Japan in Atlanta, including the Consul General (George Hisaeda) as well as Consul Orihara Shigeharu (director of the Japan Information Center), Jessica Cork (advisor for Education and Cultural Affairs), and Natasha Singh.

For their generous support of the lecture series that accompanies the exhibit, we would like to thank Catherine and Hugh Kelley and the Schultz Foundation. For his generous help with the *kanji*, we would like to thank Dr. Stephen Herschler of the Political Science Department at Oglethorpe University. For his generous help with many of the Japanese language issues, we would like to thank Dr. Robert Steen, associate professor of Japanese at Oglethorpe University. For his generous and punctilious proofreading efforts, we would like to thank Dr. Ron Carlisle. For his unerring eye for questions of style and *dharma*, we would like to thank Tom Pynn.

For her indefatigable work ethic and fierce devotion to this project, we would like to thank Lorrie King (assistant to Dr. Jason M. Wirth). For his support of the project and enduring friendship and counsel, we would like to thank Dr. David Jones (associate professor of philosophy at Kennesaw State University). For her ongoing support of the museum, we would like to thank Kitty Hodgson. For waiting so long and for miraculously making so much possible, we would like to thank Dr. Katya Vladimirov.

For their ongoing support and protection of the Oglethorpe University Museum of Art, we would like to thank the museum's Board of Directors, under the strong and able leadership of Dr. Rob Chambers. Deep thanks also go to our many friends at Clear Light Publishers for their vision and for their professionalism.

Feelings of solidarity are extended to all friends of the *dharma*, in Atlanta, in the United States, and in the world. Finally, we would like to express our heartfelt thanks to Fukushima Rōshi, to Kei San (Ikkei Kokaji), and to all of our friends at Tōfuku-ji Monastery in Kyoto.

Preface

George Hisaeda
Consul General of Japan in Atlanta

Due to great technological advancements, the world in which we live today is becoming ever smaller. With the evolution of the information age and globalization, every corner of the globe is closely linked by information, technology, capital and commodities. Therefore, the importance of understanding different cultures beyond borders is more crucial than ever. The tragic events of September 11, 2001, are a poignant reminder of this need.

This year, 2003, marks the 150th anniversary of Commodore Matthew C. Perry's first steamboat visit to Japan, which opened the door to Japan-U.S. relations. It is my great pleasure that Zen culture, one of the spiritual backbones of Japanese culture, will be exhibited here in Atlanta, the heart of the South, with calligraphy, lectures and workshops during this milestone year.

It is my sincere hope that, through this highly spiritual cultural exchange, Japan-U.S. friendship, fostered since the era of Perry's steamboats, will be deepened and strengthened, forming the foundation of friendship between our two nations for centuries to come.

Foreword

Lloyd Nick

Director, Oglethorpe University Museum of Art
Atlanta, Georgia

When Fukushima Keidō Rōshi sits quietly on the floor with a brush in his hand before he begins painting, he goes through centuries of silence, accessing the vast amount of Zen experience his mind's eye has experienced and will create.

The Zen abbot and calligrapher is a stoic sculpture, like a rock in a Zen garden, a mountain rising from and above the sea around him, communicating with himself and his past to create the ever-present now. In typically Zen fashion, time is lost into a blending of space. Only the message exists and remains. A rock coming out of the ocean mist when seen from along the shore. Mystical, inspiring, eternal. This is not only a person we admire, but a wondrous part of the world around us that is deeply instructive solely by existing.

When the trance is broken, this magician slowly changes form and becomes a spiritual brush holder guided by the brush and decades of *dokusan* (*kōan* instruction). The mind of pure spirit flows through the ink onto the pressed rice paper stretched on the floor, quietly forming the leaves of the table of Moses, the vast hidden encyclopedia of insight, the notes of the transcendent symphony. All to instruct us to a quieter and higher place.

When the last stroke is complete and spoken, a breath of air leaves like the soul leaving at the time of expiring. It has spoken, has been created, has left its mark. We have received the wisdom of the ages, the word of our own god, the sound of our inner being. For a split second, we are in tune with the universe. The image travels through the limits of our universe in our mind and into our limitless unconsciousness. Knowledge, sacred and profound, pure and mystical, pierces us like the arrow of Theresa of Avila. We have just experienced the joy of life's ode and the unveiling of its glorious and benevolent secrets.

It is with this singular cherished feeling that we introduce the extraordinary artwork of Fukushima Keidō Rōshi.

Introduction

Jason M. Wirth

In 1964, the aging and great Zen scholar D. T. Suzuki (1869–1966) came to Nanzen-ji, one of the great Rinzai Zen monasteries in Kyoto, and began attempting to convince Shibayama Rōshi (1894–1974) to replace him and come to the United States to help continue to build bridges between American culture and the Zen tradition.[1] The twentieth century with all of its wars and genocides and human disasters has been grim. Amidst all of the turmoil and tumult, the Zen tradition attempts to combat the tyranny of the ego and its regimes of suffering and hatred, ignorance and intolerance, anger and domination, with the way of wisdom and compassion. Perhaps one only knows *satori*, one only sees the moon, when the great house of the ego burns down.

Shibayama Rōshi hesitated, claiming that he was too old to come to the United States. But Suzuki Sensei, already in his mid-nineties and still overflowing with *ki*, scoffed at this, and hence Shibayama Rōshi journeyed to the United States to begin construction on a second bridge. And what a magnificent bridge it was! One of the most precious fruits of Shibayama's indefatigable bridge-building efforts remains one of the great masterpieces of Zen mind in the English language, namely, Shibayama Rōshi's *teishō* (Zen comments) on the forty-eight koans of the *Mumonkan* or *Gateless Barrier*.

Traveling with Shibayama Rōshi in 1969 was the young and irrepressibly delightful Fukushima Keidō. The Zen name Keidō means "the *dao* of joy," and in Keidō's happiness and tireless good humor and Chan Master Jōshū-like wit, one hears the playful intimations of the great and serene sea of the Zen mind.

Fukushima Rōshi later recollected that he had originally become a Zen monk for the benefit of his family. Deep Zen studies and experience taught him that "becoming a monk was not just for the sake of family, but for the whole world."[2] Indeed, Fukushima, his jokes, his

---

1. The biographical details are largely culled from Audrey Yoshiko Seo and Stephen Addiss's *The Art of Twentieth-Century Zen: Paintings and Calligraphy by Japanese Masters* (Boston: Shambhala, 1998).
2. Seo and Addiss, *op. cit.*, 178.

penetrating *teishō* and Zen lectures, and his magnificent calligraphy, all express a great and serene and freely compassionate ocean of *mushin* or Zen mind.

On the way to such wisdom and compassion, the young Fukushima found himself in 1969 in the United States for the first time. With the Sixties, of course, one thinks of things like the *Summer of Love*, love-ins, psychedelic *satori*, and other manifestations of Hippy Zen Mind. Such a mind, despite its continuous celebration of love, was remote from the compassion and wisdom of Zen mind. Already the budding bridge builder knew that part of the new, third-generation bridge would have to connect the carefree islands of Hippy Zen and New Age Relaxation Zen to the deep pure land of Zen Mind. Fukushima is a lover of bridges, visiting them whenever he has a chance, no doubt reflecting on his own compassion activity.

Fukushima Rōshi is now the Head Abbot of Tōfuku-ji Monastery, one of the five mountain monasteries (*gozan*) of Kyoto, Japan, and one of the great centers of the Rinzai Zen tradition. When the second bridge builder, Shibayama Rōshi, died in 1974, it was just a question of time before the third great Zen architect would get to work and the *dharma* would freely flow out to assuage the suffering of sentient beings.

Fukushima Rōshi, with the great ocean of his wisdom and compassion and the wild tributaries of his humor, now comes to the United States once a year. As part of those visits, Fukushima conducts demonstrations of his extraordinary calligraphy. Done in the *gyōsho* or "running, semi-cursive" style, his calligraphic inscriptions borrow from Zen's rich heritage of poetry and *Goroku* ("Records") of the sayings and activities of the great Zen Masters. Yet it would be a mistake to consider Fukushima's calligraphy as merely didactic, a gilded vessel to make Zen doctrines more palatable, as if they were sugar-coated to veil the bitter taste of their medicine. They are, of course, technically masterful, reflecting Fukushima's training in the calligraphic arts from an early age as well as his apprenticeship with Okada Rōshi and his *kaisho* or "block" script, and with Shibayama Rōshi and his exquisite *gyōsho* script. Like the beneficent force of Shibayama's calligraphy, from which he learned much, Fukushima's calligraphy is a quiet storm, a serene volcano, a compassionate and gentle eruption of the vast energy or *ki* of the Zen mind. As Fukushima explains in an interview found later in this book, "A professional calligrapher is often concerned with form—it is perhaps their greatest concern. But when a Zen Master expresses himself through calligraphy, the main purpose is the expression of Zen mind (*mushin*)." The gentle forms of Fukushima's calligraphy are rife with the erupting force of *mushin*.

It is a great privilege to have assembled in this book twenty pieces of Fukushima's callig-raphy, as well as a rare piece done by both Shibayama Rōshi and Suzuki Sensei (**Plate 22, p. 93**). Set against Fukushima's calligraphy, one can see in it all three generations of bridge builders of one of the most important lineages of *dharma* transmission from Japan to the United States. There is also a magnificent portrait of Bodhidharma (Japanese: Daruma), attributed to the incomparable Zen ink painter Sesshū Tōyō (1420–1506). Although he did not follow his teenage inclinations to cultivate the art of Zen *sumi-e* (monochrome ink paint-ing) like Sesshū, Fukushima's calligraphy is still inspired and influenced by the manner of Sesshū's ink strokes. In particular, the toenail in Sesshū's portrait of the standing Daruma can still be seen in the final stroke in Fukushima's signature on his calligraphy.[3]

It is also an honor to collect in this volume essays on Fukushima in particular and Zen calligraphy in general by some of the leading scholars in the field. Dr. Audrey Yoshiko Seo, principal author of *The Art of Twentieth-Century Zen: Paintings and Calligraphy by Japanese Masters*, provides an intellectual biography of Fukushima. Dr. Stephen Addiss, a preeminent scholar in this field and author of, among numerous other works, *The Art of Zen*, provides an invaluable guide to the fundamentals of appreciating both Zen calligraphy in general and the works in this book in particular. Dr. Stephen J. Goldberg provides an important set of philo-sophical and art historical considerations in approaching works of Zen calligraphy. I provide some philosophical perspectives of my own, and Dr. Ronald L. Carlisle offers a brief history of Tōfuku-ji Monastery. Also included is an interview with Fukushima Rōshi, accompanied by an interpreter, Jeff Shore (professor of Zen Buddhism at Hanazono University in Kyoto), which I conducted at Tōfuku-ji in November 2001. In the appendix are short biographies of Okada Rōshi, Shibayama Rōshi and Fukushima Rōshi.

Finally this book is an homage to Fukushima Keidō Rōshi, in deepest appreciation for his friendship, his art, his Zen training, his indefatigable *dharma* teaching, and his deep and gen-erous Zen mind.

---

3. A more detailed discussion of this influence can be found in Stephen Addiss's essay. Vide Plate 21, p. 89.

Fukushima Keidō Rōshi in America. Photo © Ron Carlisle.

Fukushima Keidō

REFLECTIONS IN INK

Audrey Yoshiko Seo

In Asia, the art of calligraphy is believed to reveal one's true spirit and nature. In the fluid lines, gentle curves, and sharp angles of ink there lies a reflection of personal experiences long passed. In the case of Fukushima Keidō (born 1933), Zen Master and Head Abbot of Tōfuku-ji Monastery in Kyoto, the personal experiences and memories associated with his development as a calligrapher and Zen Master go back to childhood and are both joyous and sad.

"My grandmother was a good calligrapher," he states. "She wrote both *kanji* (Chinese characters) and *kana* (Japanese script). When I was about seven years old, she told me to practice calligraphy." At this point, Fukushima Rōshi had not yet developed a full appreciation of the art, and like most seven-year-olds, preferred to spend his time riding his bicycle. "To practice calligraphy you have to sit straight and make ink correctly. I already did not like this part. I couldn't make good ink—it just blurred when I wrote." His best friend, Susumu, didn't have a bicycle, but enjoyed practicing calligraphy and could make good ink. "Susumu would do two pieces of calligraphy and, in exchange for one of them, I would let him ride my bicycle home from our calligraphy lessons. Then I would show Susumu's calligraphy to my grandmother. But my grandmother always knew, and she would say, 'Next time, please do it yourself.'" [1]

---

1. Unless otherwise noted, stories about Fukushima Rōshi's childhood and his early calligraphic studies are from an interview with him at Tōfuku-ji in May 2001.

In the fourth grade, Fukushima Rōshi wrote the character *"ki"* 器 ("instrument, tool, utensil"; also "capacity, ability"), which is a difficult character for many people to write because of its particular balance and structure. His teacher said his character was very good and marked it with many red circles, a sign of praise in East Asian schools. Fukushima Rōshi eagerly showed the work to his grandmother, who said proudly, "You *can* do good calligraphy." From that point Fukushima, then about ten years old, had more self-confidence in his ability and began to really enjoy practicing brushwork.

Fukushima Rōshi attended school in Kobe City, where annually one student's calligraphy was chosen to hang in the town shrine. During his fifth and sixth years of school, Fukushima Rōshi's calligraphy was selected twice. As he entered junior high school at the age of twelve, his grandmother continued to be a great influence on him. When Fukushima Rōshi asked his grandmother to buy him a dictionary of Japanese literature, she said, "You do not need one, please ask me your questions." His grandmother was not only a severe critic of calligraphy, but was also well read and had graduated from junior high—rare for a woman of her day.

During the war, Kobe City was bombed several times by U.S. forces. The first time, the houses of Fukushima's family and his friend Susumu's family remained unharmed. The second time, both houses were destroyed. Fukushima Rōshi's family had managed to escape to the hillside, but Fukushima Rōshi never saw his friend Susumu or his friend's family again.

Fukushima Rōshi's sister passed away when he was twelve and his grandmother died the following year. Fukushima decided to become a Buddhist monk so that they would go to paradise. He cut off ties with his family at the age of fourteen and entered Hōfuku-ji Temple in Okayama, but Fukushima still had to finish junior high school. He divided his time between school studies and temple duties, but these kept him quite busy, and he no longer had time to practice calligraphy. However, when his Master, Okada Kidō Rōshi, was away from the temple, Fukushima would sit in front of paintings by the great Muromachi Period (1336–1573) ink painter Sesshū Tōyō (1420–1506), which the temple owned. Seeing works by Sesshū, known for his innovative compositions and strong brushwork, made a lasting impression on the young monk:

> From the age of fourteen I grew up looking at the works of
> Sesshū. I remember very clearly the moment when I saw

Sesshū's painting for the first time. We were expecting a special guest, and only when a guest would come was a painting by Sesshū exhibited. Therefore my Master took the scroll out of the storage room and carefully hung it in the *tokonoma*. My Master said, "This is a National Treasure by Sesshū." I thought, "If this is all, then I can paint this myself too." That was because at that time, I didn't understand the depth of Sesshū's painting yet. After studying Zen and training, I gradually understood the depth of Sesshū's painting. I also understood the beauty of space in his painting, so as I grew up and lived surrounded by Sesshū's work I began to understand painting.[2]

Young Fukushima was especially fascinated by a painting of a standing Bodhidharma (**Plate 21, p. 88**). He would sometimes secretly take the painting out and copy the sharp lines of the toes. Today Fukushima Rōshi believes the influence of Sesshū's lines are present in each of his own calligraphies.[3]

Fukushima, now in his early teens, would often assist Okada Rōshi when he did calligraphy by making the ink and preparing the paper. "Seeing fine calligraphy is good for practice," explains Fukushima Rōshi. He developed an appreciation for Okada's "hard style" of standard script (*kaisho*) brushwork, and later while a graduate student wrote in almost the same style as his Master. Gradually, his own personal style began to soften, and he now prefers the "running" or semi-cursive (*gyōsho*) style.

Fukushima remembers another favorite story from that time. In 1950 there was an exhibition of American culture in a baseball stadium in Nishinomiya, outside Kobe. Fukushima's mother was fond of the United States and she sent a letter to Hōfuku-ji asking Okada Rōshi if it would be possible for teenage Fukushima to come see the exhibition with her and his younger half-brother, who is now also a monk. Okada Rōshi agreed to let Fukushima Rōshi go to the exhibition, which contained American automobiles, airplanes and even blue jeans.

---

2. Fukushima Keidō, from the introduction to his calligraphy demonstration, University of Richmond, March 1996.

3. Fukushima also noted that while he was later training at Nanzen-ji under Shibayama Rōshi he took an interest in sharp lines of calligraphy by Tōgo Heihachirō (1848–1934), who had won the naval war against Russia in 1905, and also in the letters of the famous leader Date Masamune (1567–1636).

Okada Rōshi

Fukushima had already studied about American democracy in school, but here was a firsthand look at its culture. From that point Fukushima developed his great appreciation for America. As a souvenir of the trip to the exhibition, Fukushima's mother bought him a pair of blue jeans so he could wear them while doing work at the temple. They were so long he had to roll up the cuffs. The other young monks at Hōfuku-ji really liked the blue jeans, but Okada Rōshi became angry since they were Western style, not Japanese. Fukushima Rōshi still has those jeans packed away in a box he brought back to Kyoto from Okayama. This early introduction to American culture, including his attempt to incorporate Western blue jeans into temple life, would reveal itself again later in Fukushima's experiences as a Zen teacher.

When Fukushima was in his third year of high school, Shibayama Zenkei Rōshi (1894–1974) visited Hōfuku-ji from Nanzen-ji Temple in Kyoto. During the visit, Okada and Shibayama discussed plans for Fukushima's college education, and it was decided that he should attend Ōtani University in Kyoto, where Shibayama had lectured and D. T. Suzuki had taught. Fukushima Rōshi eventually enrolled at Ōtani, studying Indian Buddhism, and continuing with graduate studies in Chinese Buddhism and Zen, focusing on the *Rinzai Roku* (*Record of Rinzai*) for his thesis. He had planned to become a scholar of Buddhist studies, but understood that in order truly to understand Zen, he would have to practice it. So he decided to enter Shibayama Rōshi's training hall at Nanzen-ji, making a three-year commitment for the sake of his scholarly pursuits. In the end, he trained with Shibayama for ten and a half years.[4] Shibayama and Okada had both been disciples of Kōno Rōshi, but their personalities

---

4. For a more complete discussion of Fukishima Rōshi's life, Zen training and calligraphy, see "Bridges of Zen: Shibayama Zenkei and Fukushima Keidō" in *The Art of Twentieth-Century Zen* by Audrey Yoshiko Seo with Stephen Addiss (Boston: Shambhala, 1998), 167–91.

were vastly different. Okada Rōshi was strict while Shibayama was more gentle; Fukushima was absorbing important aspects from both Masters:

> Their personalities were totally different. Okada was very severe; Shibayama was very elegant; I respected both of them. In the beginning of one's training one needs a more severe Master. But to become a complete, full-fledged Zen Master it is important to not only have the strict side, but also the gentle side, especially when teaching laypeople. But even Rōshi Shibayama was very severe during *kōan* study. I was very fortunate to begin with a strict Master and then gentle Master. If it had been the other way, I would not have gotten the basics down.[5]

Fukushima Rōshi completed his *kōan* training under Shibayama in 1968. The following year he accompanied his Master to the United States for the first time. Shibayama had been traveling to the United States since 1965 at the behest of D. T. Suzuki, who had retired from his position as a lecturer at Columbia University, but who felt that maintaining a relationship between the U.S. and Japanese Zen was important. Shibayama Rōshi visited the United States a total of eight times, lecturing and giving meditation sessions.

During the 1969 trip, Fukushima encountered American hippies experimenting with all forms of New Age philosophies and psychedelic substances, seeking some form of enlightenment. American interest in Zen was beginning to flourish, and Fukushima reconnected with the American culture he was first introduced to by his mother two decades earlier.

Then in 1973, at the urging of Shibayama Rōshi, Fukushima Rōshi spent a year at Claremont College in California as a guest lecturer on Zen. The trip was viewed by Shibayama as a modern *angya* (pilgrimage). At Claremont, Fukushima gave Zen lectures in English and held meditation sessions. The experience seems to have had a profound effect on his approach to teaching Zen and cultural understanding, and further cemented his bonds with American culture.

---

5. Interview with Fukushima Keidō, March 1997, Richmond, Virginia.

Unconsciously I became more open. For instance, everyone has his or her own ideas about the world, religion, life. That year I had a big change; it was a good experience for me to stay in the United States. My duties were just to teach Zen and meditation, so I concentrated on teaching. For instance, by learning which Zen stories are most effective for Americans, I concentrated on how to teach Zen to Americans. Even now, my ideas of teaching Zen come from that time. Even in Japan, my ideas of opening outward are apparent; I encourage Japanese young people to leave Japan, and look at their own country from outside.[6]

The following year Fukushima returned to Hōfuku-ji to assist Okada Rōshi. At that time three Americans arrived asking to become disciples. Although the Americans did not remain at the temple permanently, they became Fukushima's first American followers.

In the fall of 1980, Fukushima became Zen Master at Tōfuku-ji. At the time, the monastery had no monks in training, a fact Fukushima mentioned to one of his American disciples, who promptly traveled to Japan and entered the monastery. Eventually three Japanese monks entered the training hall, supervised by the American who actually had more Zen experience. By the spring, nine more monks entered the monastery, and in 1987 there were twenty-five. This was an unusual episode in the history of one of Japan's oldest and most prestigious Zen temples, but all part of the changing face of Zen.

The temple, now revitalized by the forward-thinking Fukushima Rōshi, continued to be rejuvenated. Throughout the 1980s requests came from universities for Fukushima to return to the United States and lecture, but his increasingly demanding schedule and monastic duties forced him to decline the invitations. Then in 1989 a request came from Stephen Addiss to serve as an "artist in residence" during the exhibition *The Art of Zen: Paintings and Calligraphy by Japanese Zen Monks, 1600–1925*. Fukushima Rōshi was asked to give Zen lectures, meditation sessions, and, most significantly, calligraphy demonstrations to help the

---

6. Interview with Fukushima Keidō at Tōfuku-ji, May 1997.

Shibayama Rōshi

general public better understand the artwork. The monastery was running smoothly, and Fukushima Rōshi believed the time was right to return to the United States. During his ten-day stay as artist in residence, he gave his first public calligraphy demonstration, something that is not done by monks in Japan. "During the question and answer period there were many good questions about Japanese culture, so I realized the meaning of the demonstration: instead of static calligraphy, it is living, dynamic, moving art."[7]

As he had done as a young monk under Okada Rōshi at Hōfuku-ji, Fukushima had also assisted Shibayama Rōshi during his calligraphy sessions. "I realized Rōshi Shibayama's specialty is rhythm. I had already studied the rhythm by watching, and when I did calligraphy, my own rhythm came out. I never thought about fast or slow, it just naturally emerged due to *mushin*" (**Plate 4, p. 25**). Fukushima Rōshi added, "When I helped Rōshi Shibayama do calligraphy, at first it was not rhythmic. But gradually the rhythm came, then finally the rhythm would be in his whole body, then he started humming. I would start humming too. Eventually I forgot the song."

This experience from many years ago would return unexpectedly as a part of Fukushima's own calligraphy practice. Today at Tōfuku-ji, Fukushima Rōshi does calligraphy alone in a back room of the temple where only the senior monks are allowed to enter. One day, a senior monk noticed that Fukushima Rōshi was humming while he was doing brushwork. When the monk pointed this out, Fukushima Rōshi was surprised, not realizing he had been doing it. Fukushima Rōshi asked the monk what tune he had been humming. The monk hummed the tune. It was the American national anthem, the same tune Shibayama Rōshi used to hum.

---

7. Introduction to a calligraphy demonstration, University of Richmond, March 1996.

Fukushima Rōshi sees his calligraphic style coming out of Shibayama Rōshi's influence, which comes largely from the work of Jiun Sonja (1781–1804), whose blunt, energetic style of calligraphy Shibayama Rōshi greatly admired and emulated. Today, Fukushima Rōshi has his larger calligraphy brushes custom-made with short, stubby tips to recreate the style. Fukushima Rōshi also admires the work of Hakuin Ekaku (1686–1769), Sengai Gibon (1750–1837) and more recently Furukawa Taikō (1872–1968) of Myōshin-ji. "Of the last generation, there were many Zen Masters who did calligraphy, but Shibayama and Furukawa were the best. Furukawa's brushwork was very skillful because at that time, he used only the brush in daily life." Asked if there are any distinctions between professional and Zen calligraphy, Fukushima Rōshi explained, "All Zen Masters can do calligraphy with a Zen mind, but as an art, sometimes it is not skillful because they did not do the fundamental practice of calligraphy. Zen Masters should do fundamental practice of calligraphy before training as a monk." Fukushima Rōshi explained the unique distinction of Zen calligraphy more fully at one of his calligraphy demonstrations:

> In the calligraphy of a Zen Master the right Zen mind must be contained. There is also calligraphy in which the art is not very good. That is proof that the Master has not done much calligraphy. But one can still see the Zen mind there. This is a characteristic of Zen calligraphy. In some cases the person has expressed his Zen mind by drawing only one line; after I had explained this at one university, I was asked, "Looking at your calligraphy, where is your Zen mind?" Actually, from the point of picking up the brush, everything is Zen mind, it is not in only one point. The total thing is Zen mind.[8]

The art of calligraphy has become increasingly popular and appreciated in the West, in part due to the influence of abstract expressionist painting and an expanding interest in Eastern philosophies and culture. Thanks to Fukushima Rōshi's numerous visits to the

---

8. Fukushima Keidō, from introductory lecture to a calligraphy demonstration, University of Richmond, March 1996.

United States, which feature public calligraphy demonstrations, Americans have had the opportunity to see a Zen Master create art reflecting his Zen mind and experience. But is it possible for the layperson to see the Zen mind in calligraphy? "Lay people who study Zen can see the Zen mind. When you see a calligraphy by Hakuin, you not only see the Zen mind, but also the power." Fukushima's bold calligraphic works draw the viewers in and pique their interest and curiosity about Zen, an effect that he responds to with great joy and satisfaction.

Although Fukushima Rōshi has become a noted Zen calligrapher in Japan, and also in the United States thanks to his many visits, he does not paint images. Despite studying Sesshū paintings as a young monk, and despite the fact that Shibayama Rōshi painted numerous subjects, Fukushima prefers to stick with calligraphy. But before becoming a Zen Master, he used to practice images of Daruma, and recently a senior Zen Master asked Fukushima for a painting of Daruma. Fukushima Rōshi declined the request, but another Zen Master said, "It's easy, just two circles on top of each other." Fukushima Rōshi painted two circles on a *shikishi* (poem card) and sent it to him. The other Zen Master asked, "Is that a Daruma?"[9]

Fukushima Rōshi recently returned to Hōfuku-ji Temple in Okayama and looked at the Sesshū painting of Bodhidharma that had affected him so strongly as a fourteen-year-old-monk. Hōfuku-ji owns ten paintings by Sesshū, five of which have been designated National Treasures. The Bodhidharma painting is not a National Treasure, but Fukushima Rōshi likes it best because of its powerful presence and sharp lines. The lines that impressed him as a young monk just coming to terms with his calligraphy practice are transformed into the lines that can be seen today in his own calligraphy.

---

9. This simplified approach to the Daruma image refers to Daruma seated in meditation in front of a wall for nine years in China. Some images are composed of only a single-stroke outline of the figure and are referred to as *ippitsu Daruma* ("one-stroke Daruma"). See the example by Nantenbō in *The Art of Twentieth-Century Zen*, 28 (plate 8).

The Calligraphic Works of Fukushima Keidō

Stephen Addiss

Japanese Calligraphy

Zen Buddhism traveled to Japan from China, and with it came a tradition of ink painting and calligraphy that also had roots in the Chinese literati tradition. Because of this background, it may not be surprising that most Zen calligraphy in Japan is written in Chinese, rather than Japanese, which adds simplified *kana* syllabary to Chinese *kanji* characters. Even today in secular circles, the appeal of the more than 50,000 Chinese characters, each a word in itself, is such that at least half of Japanese calligraphy is written in Chinese. Of course, these characters are also used in writing Japanese, along with *kana* for verb and adjectival endings, prepositions, and other uses. But the pure use of *kanji*, in any one of five different script forms and allowing for innumerable personal variations, remains the art form of choice for many thousands of Japanese amateur as well as professional calligraphers.

Zen Masters, despite their high degree of artistry, rank among the amateurs since they create their calligraphic works to be given to monks and lay followers. This also follows the Chinese literati tradition, where selling one's works was considered a possible impediment to

Plate 1. Fukushima Keidō, *Mu*, ink on paper, 13.5" x 53".

無

the integrity of creating from one's inner spirit. In the West we do not have such respect for non-professional art, but since the word amateur comes from "love," it is not surprising that in East Asia the non-professional literati and Zen traditions developed to high degrees of both quality and appreciation. This was especially true because it has long been believed that the flexible brush cannot help but reveal the inner character of the calligrapher, and viewing a work is tantamount to having the monk/scholar/poet/artist in your presence. The works of Fukushima Keidō Rōshi therefore exemplify both his individual personality and his Zen mind.

A few general principles can help the first-time viewer of calligraphy. Whether printed or written, Chinese and Japanese texts begin at the top right and move down in vertical columns from right to left. The characters themselves consist of from one to several dozen strokes, which follow traditional brush movement (the horizontals begin on the left, the verticals at the top), and a traditional order in which the strokes are made. The general rule is each character is written from left to right, and from top to bottom. When viewing a calligraphy, therefore, we may follow the movement of the brush, now straight, now turning, now quick, now slower. In this way we can recreate the work in our minds, unlike viewing most paintings where we cannot know which area may have been done first. Calligraphy is an art that can be compared to music, moving through time, or even more closely compared to dance, moving through both time and space.

The calligrapher has an abundance of choices to make before beginning a work, including text, style, format, size, and script. Of the five basic Chinese scripts, two are somewhat archaic. The ancient "seal script" is now mostly used for carving characters into seals (sometimes called *chops*) because this script emphasizes even lines, balance, and control. "Clerical script," developed 2,000 years ago, is somewhat akin to our Gothic script (𝔜𝔢 𝔒𝔩𝔡𝔢 𝔗𝔢𝔞 𝔖𝔥𝔬𝔭𝔭𝔢), and similarly is now mostly utilized to give an elegant and old-fashioned flavor. The three remaining scripts might be compared to our standard, running, and cursive scripts: printed, written, and dashed off very quickly. For example, we seldom write the small *a* the way it is printed. Instead, we tend to simplify and connect some of our strokes with the pen together in running script; when we join all the letters in rapid order, we can call our script cursive. This can be difficult to read at times, but imagine if, instead of twenty-six letter possibilities, we had more than 50,000 shapes—this is the task of reading cursive script in Chinese.

Figure 1. The word *Mu* in five scripts and different styles.

It surprises many Westerners to find out that relatively few educated Chinese and Japanese can completely decipher calligraphy in cursive script, but this is one of the indications that reading the calligraphy is not essential to its appreciation. An ordinary text written beautifully is fine visual art, and a magnificent text written poorly is not, so in some ways those who cannot read the script have an advantage. They can look at the calligraphy as line, form, and movement within positive and negative space, and see the artistic merits of the work without being sidetracked by trying to read each character. There are translations of all the works in this book, so readers can consider these scrolls both as artistic forms and as Zen statements. In both cases, they are a form of Zen teaching.

Fukushima Rōshi's Calligraphy

The Zen Master Fukushima almost always writes his calligraphy in running-cursive script, tending towards fully cursive. That means that the strokes in his characters are simplified and joined together, so that the character *mu* (**Plate 1, p. 14**), which ordinarily takes twelve strokes of the brush (**Figure 1, this page**), is completed in one gesture. It seems fitting that this word for "no/not/nothing" that is so important in Zen training becomes a single form in his calligraphy. *Mu* is often the first *kōan* (Zen conundrum) given to Zen students once they have meditated enough to quiet their minds. The Zen Master Chao-chou (Japanese: Jōshū, 778–897) was asked by a pupil, "Does a dog have Buddha-nature?" Since Buddhists believe that all living beings have Buddha-nature, the obvious answer would be yes, but instead Jōshū said, "*Mu*."

What is *mu*? Zen students may meditate on this *kōan* for weeks, months, or years, seeking a breakthrough towards enlightenment. The Zen Master Hakuin (1686–1769) wrote that when he finally penetrated this *kōan* it was like an endless sheet of ice breaking.[1] Fukushima feels a special sense of connection with Jōshū, and he frequently writes *mu* in cursive script as a one-word calligraphy. He prefers the word not to be translated, but to become in itself a word in English. Viewing this calligraphy, we can sense how Fukushima has started with a strong horizontal stroke, paused slightly, then moved the brush in strong curving motions until the character ends with "flying white" at the bottom. This term indicates that some of the white of the paper shows through the brushstroke, and is caused by the brush beginning to become dry of ink, or rapid brush movement, or (as in this case) both. Underneath the single word, Fukushima signs his work *Tōfuku Kanshō Kōyū Dōnin* (Head Abbot of Tōfuku-ji Kōyū, *Man of the Way*). The two diagonal strokes at the end of each column of the signature are transformations of the Sesshū "toe" brushstrokes that impressed Fukushima as a young monk (**Plate 21, p. 89**). To complete the work, Fukushima has added an opening seal at the top right and two final seals at the lower left. These are chosen from the vast array of seals that he owns; the opening seal usually has a motto such as "True Sect of Rinzai," while the lower seals bear his Zen names.

Another variation of what is sometimes called a "one-word barrier" calligraphy is shown in **Plate 2, opposite page**. The large word at the top is *totsu*, a Zen shout, and below it there is a three-word inscription; Fukushima translates the entire work as "Hey, throw it away!" The large *totsu* is composed of two parts, originally a small square representing a mouth on the left and the graph meaning "go out" on the right; together they indicate the shout. Fukushima has connected the brushstrokes, making the word more difficult to read but adding a sense of unified strength. Not only is the character bursting with asymmetrical power, but the empty areas around it are also energized, such as the fascinating negative space on its lower left. This takes place because *totsu* is written with a continuous and energized

---

1. Vide *The Zen Master Hakuin*, trans. Philip B. Yampolsky (New York: Columbia University Press, 1971), 118.

Plate 2. Fukushima Keidō, *Hey, Throw It Away*, ink on paper, 13.5" x 53".

咄　放下著

少

救心苦

上福岩寺文

文金堂人

Figure 2. The word *under* in five scripts and various styles.

combination of straight and curved lines, as well as quicker and slower brush movements, and like the previous *mu*, it ends with a diagonal/vertical line showing "flying white."

Underneath *totsu*, the three characters of the inscription "throw it away" are written in smaller size but with equal energy; the middle word (usually translated "below," see **Figure 2, at left**), is here transformed into three dots. Fukushima's signature and final seals now occupy a single column on the left; placement of these elements is a vital part of the entire work's composition. While *totsu* is best known as the shout of the Zen Master Lin-chi (Japanese: Rinzai, died 867), the next phrase comes from a story about Jōshū. A monk asked, "What about when I don't have anything?" The Master said, "Throw it away."[2]

The third "one-word barrier" in this book is, appropriately, a powerfully architectonic rendition of the word *kan* that means "barrier" and has a pictorial origin as a gate (**Plate 3, p. 23**). The Zen Master Wu-men (Japanese: Mumon, 1183–1260) wrote, "In studying Zen, one must pass the barriers set up by ancient Zen Masters. For the attainment of incomparable *satori*, one has to cast aside his discriminating mind."[3] This directly leads to the following Fukushima calligraphy, *Mushin* (**Plate 4, p. 25**). *Mu* is visibly the same character as in **Plate 1 (p. 14)**, and the second word of the compound, *shin*, means "mind" or "heart." This two-word phrase, which Fukushima also prefers not to translate, is extremely important in Zen teaching. One could try to explain *mushin*, but it is a Zen practice rather than an intellectual concept—since art has

---

2. From *The Recorded Sayings of Zen Master Jōshū*, trans. James Green (Boston: Shambhala Publications, 1998), 121 (section 382). In another Zen text entitled "Compendium of the Five Lamps," the story continues: The monk then asked, "I don't have anything, what is there to throw away?" Jōshū answered, "In that case, take it with you."

3. Quoted in Zenkei Shibayama, *Zen Comments on the Mumonkan*, trans. Sumiko Kudo (New York: Harper & Row, 1974), 19.

the potentiality to go beyond words, perhaps the meaning of *mushin* can be felt, at least in part, by examining Fukushima's calligraphy written with Zen mind.

Another two-word calligraphy by Fukushima is *Pure and Empty* (**Plate 5, p. 27**), written horizontally rather than vertically. The character "pure" on the right is composed of a "water" radical on the left and "blue" on the right, and we can imagine how the ancient Chinese found the concept of purity in clear blue water. This work exemplifies how Fukushima's style combines fluency with strength. Most cursive script over the centuries has been written with thinner and more curved strokes of the brush, giving a feeling of flying lightly over the paper or silk. Instead, Fukushima's style is more massive, with a great deal of "bone" (structure) as well as "flesh" (surface appeal). As he says, he learned this style from his teacher Shibayama Rōshi (**Plate 22, p. 93**) while assisting and watching him doing calligraphy. On the rare occasions when Fukushima writes in standard script, he follows his other teacher Okada Rōshi (**Plate 23, p. 97**), but most of his work is in the Shibayama tradition.[4]

As noted in the essay by Professor Seo, Shibayama Rōshi was very attracted to the works of the Shingon monk Jiun Sonja (1718–1804), who also studied Zen and is often included in exhibitions of Zen art. Jiun's style is broad, strong, and rough, with a frequent use of "flying white." He may have used a brush made of split bamboo to create some of his works, and since he was a great scholar of Indian Buddhist texts, his writing of Sanskrit may also have influenced his calligraphy. The main characteristics of Jiun's calligraphy are evident in his two-character work *Fumai* (*Not Deluded*, **Figure 3, p. 30**). The strokes of the brush are even rougher than those of Shibayama, and there is more "flying white," but the massive boldness and asymmetrical sense of balance are similar. Here the first (right-hand) character *fu* is a common word for "not." The second character, *mai,* is composed of a left-hand "sun" radical and a form on the right meaning "not yet." The word often indicates "dark" (not yet sunny) and also carries the meanings of foolish or deluded.

A rare example of a calligraphy by Shibayama together with the Zen scholar D. T. Suzuki (1869–1966) is shown in **Plate 22, p. 93**. The large character on the right is *myō* ("wondrous") written by Suzuki with rough "flying white" brushwork and linear force and ending with a

---

4. For more biographical information and further examples of the calligraphy of Shibayama and Fukushima, see Audrey Yoshiko Seo, with Stephen Addiss, *The Art of Twentieth-Century Zen* (Boston: Shambhala, 1998), 167–91.

Figure 3. Jiun Sonja (1718–1804), *Not Deluded*, ink on paper, 34.6 x 52 cm., private collection.

strong diagonal. To the left is a five-word inscription, "Making fire in water," written in more rounded brushstrokes by Shibayama. The work was created on October 10, 1964, when Suzuki visited Shibayama at Nanzen-ji in Kyoto. A few months later, Suzuki returned to Nanzen-ji and persuaded Shibayama to make his first trip to the United States, taking along a young monk named Fukushima.[5]

Moving to three-character calligraphy, the first two examples by Fukushima are *Bright and Clear* (**Plate 6, p. 30**) and *Appear with Dignity* (**Plate 7, p. 33**). Both of these have the second character repeat as the third, which Fukushima indicates with a "repeat" sign that is simpler in form than the characters above it, and both works are expressions of *satori* enlightenment. The word for "bright" in the former scroll is composed of a "sun" on the left and a "moon" on the right, although the pictographic elements are less visible in the powerful cursive script.

---

5. For further details, vide *ibid.*, 167 and 171–2.

Plate 3. Fukushima Keidō, *Barrier*, ink on paper, 13.5" x 53".

関

A final three-word phrase comes from Jōshū, *Go Have Some Tea* (**Plate 11, p. 41**). The story has the Master questioning two newly arrived monks. He asked the first, "Have you been here before?" The monk replied, "No, I haven't." The Master said, "Go have some tea." He then asked the second monk, "Have you been here before?" The monk answered, "Yes, I have." The Master said, "Go have some tea." The head monk now asked the Master, "Setting aside that you told the monk who had not been here to have some tea, why did you tell the monk who had already been here to have some tea?" The Master said, "Go have some tea."[6]

Of the four-word phrases in this book, **Plate 9, p. 37**, is especially significant as the words of the semi-legendary First Patriarch Bodhidharma (Japanese: Daruma) who brought Zen from India to China in the late fifth or early sixth century. It forms the second of three phrases spoken to Emperor Wu in South China. First the Emperor asked how much merit he had achieved by endowing Buddhist temples and ordinations. Daruma replied "No merit." Asked by the Emperor about his doctrine, Daruma responded with the words Fukushima chose for this calligraphy, "Vast emptiness, nothing sacred." We can recognize here the third character as *mu*, and also note how Fukushima has written the first word so it ends moving down to the second, which closes the space with a strong horizontal. The third and fourth words have the same basic composition, thus clearly indicating the four characters as a pair of two-word phrases.

The story continues that the Emperor failed to understand, and asked, "Who is this confronting me?" Daruma replied "*Fushiki*" ("I don't know"), which Fukushima has written as his third two-word calligraphy in this collection (**Plate 10, p. 39**). Here *fu* ("not") is the same four-stroke word seen in the Jiun calligraphy, while *shiki* ("know," "discriminate") is a character that requires eighteen strokes in standard script. As can be seen in this scroll, complex characters are more abbreviated in cursive script than simple ones, leading to a sense of artistic balance. To complete the story, after this cryptic remark Daruma left the Emperor, moved onwards to Northern China, and subsequently meditated for nine years in front of a wall. A Chinese monk who eventually became his successor and the second patriarch then

---

6. Adapted from *The Recorded Sayings of Zen Master Jōshū, op. cit.*, 146 (section 459).

Plate 4. Fukushima Keidō, *Mushin*, ink on paper, 13.5" x 53".

無心

approached him. Zen has continued to the present through teacher-to-student training, including the use of *kōan* such as "*Fushiki.*"

One of the most famous *kōan* comes from the Master Yun-men (Japanese: Ummon, died 949), speaking to his Zen students. "I don't ask you about before the fifteenth day, but try to say something about after the fifteenth day." He then answered for them, "Every day is a good day."[7] Literally the five words in this phrase are "Day day this good day" (**Plate 12, p. 45**). The pictographic character for "sun" also means "day," and it occurs three times in the five words. Avoiding direct repetition of form, Fukushima writes "day" at the top in its usual square form with a dot inside (the form was round in its ancient origin), then uses a repeat sign for the second character, and finally makes the fifth word an unusual and creative variation in a triangular shape. This may suggest that every day is good, but each day is also different.

Two scrolls in this book are composed of paired phrases in the Chinese poetic idiom of five words for each line. **Plate 15, p. 59** has the couplet:

> Old pines speak wisdom (*hannya*);
> Hidden birds whisper truth.

Both phrases use images from nature to allude to *satori*, a frequent practice in Zen where the outer world is not separate from the inner. The scroll is written to give a second visual rhythm to that of the five-five characters. In this arrangement, the first column is made up of seven words, the second only three, and the work is then asymmetrically balanced by Fukushima's signature line in smaller script. However, Fukushima indicates the beginnings of the poetic lines with bolder brushwork, first for the "old" that opens the scroll, and then for the penultimate character in the first column, "hidden," with its powerful dot seeming to fly off to the right.

---

7. This *kōan* is included in *The Blue Cliff Record* (Japanese: *Hekiganroku*, trans. Thomas Cleary and J. C. Cleary (Boston: Shambhala, 1977), 37–45 (case 6).

Plate 5. Fukushima Keidō, *Pure and Empty*, ink on paper, 13.5" x 53".

清虚

Four of Fukushima's works in this book are *ensō*, a word meaning circle. There is some debate as to whether *ensō* are paintings or calligraphy. On one hand, they are almost always created by a single calligraphic line,[8] but on the other hand, they do not directly represent a word. Perhaps they form a category of their own, and *ensō* by Zen Masters have a long history of creation and appreciation. Fukushima emphasizes that an *ensō* becomes a Zen circle only with the addition of an inscription, and in these four works he has added four different phrases.

The first Fukushima *ensō* is a horizontal work with a traditional three-word inscription, "What is this?" (**Plate 17, p. 67**). Since the Zen circle has had interpretations including the universe, nothingness, the moon, or even a rice-cake, it is clearly up to each viewer to make his/her own interpretation. The circle itself is broad and luminous, and unlike other Zen artists of the past, Fukushima puts his opening seal (reading "Rinzai True Sect") right in its center, as he explains "the act of a free Zen mind."

A second *ensō* is inscribed with a seven-word poetic phrase, "There are flowers, there is the moon, there is a pavilion" (**Plate 18, p. 78**). Since viewings of cherry blossoms or the moon are favorite activities in Japan, often taking place from a pavilion, this inscription has some affinities with "Every day is a good day." Is the circle here the moon, a blossom, or perhaps the total experience?

The third Fukushima *ensō* carries an important three-word Zen phrase, "No guest or host" (**Plate 19, p. 83**). There is a strong East Asian tradition of guest and host, not only in activities such as the tea ceremony, but also in Zen. The Master Lin-chi discussed the four positions of host and guest: host as host, guest as guest, host amidst guest, guest amidst host. There are also two stories about Jōshū involving this concept. In the first, a monk asked, "What is the host amidst the guest?" The Master said, "I do not ask for a wife." The monk asked, "What is the guest amidst the host?" The Master said, "I have no father-in-law."[9]

The second story alludes to monks in training being compared with drifting white clouds. A monk asked, "What about it when the white clouds do not fade away?" Jōshū said, "I don't know anything about meteorology." The monk said, "Are there no host and guest?"

---

8. For an example of a rare two-stroke *ensō*, vide Stephen Addiss, *The Art of Zen* (New York: Harry N. Abrams, 1989), 73.
9. From *The Recorded Sayings of Zen Master Jōshū*, *op. cit.*, 18 (section 20).

The Master said, "I am host, you are guest. What are the white clouds?"[10] Jōshū is here instructing a monk pupil, but in Fukushima's calligraphy, we go beyond even these important distinctions: "No guest or host." The first word of this inscription is *mu*, so a secondary interpretation could be "*Mu* guest and host." We may also note that while the penultimate word *guest* is rather open in format, the final character host is created in a triangular shape, ending with a broad horizontal line that effectively concludes the total composition.

The final *ensō* in this book has Fukushima's original inscription in English, "Watch, touch and bite" (**Plate 20, p. 87**). Each verb is more active than the previous one, but what does this *ensō* mean? Once again the viewer must become a part of the experience, for it is a question of seeing rather than just looking. In this work, as in all the scrolls on view, Fukushima Rōshi invites us to participate, to share the Zen mind that he has imbued in the artistry of putting brush and ink to paper. Then there will indeed be no guest or host.

---

10. *Ibid.*, 50–51 (section 124).

Recognition of the True Self
ZEN BUDDHISM & *BOKUSEKI* CALLIGRAPHY

Stephen J. Goldberg

The Chinese "art of writing," *Shufa* 書法 , commonly referred to in the West as "calligraphy," addresses us across generations and geographies as the material expression of an interlocutor from the past. It appeals to us visually, and the performance of its brushstrokes as inscription of an originary gesture elicits *zhiji* 知己, "recognition of the true self." This is referred to in traditional writings on calligraphy as *xinyin* 心印 or "inscription of the heart-mind." *Xin* 心 (Japanese: *kokoro*), or "heart-mind," is a non-dualistic conception of the embodied human subject. At issue is precisely how recognition (*zhi* 知)—the basic relation we have with others and the world—functions in a distinctive way within calligraphy. Interpreted within the context of traditional Chinese culture, these "signs of self" are motivated by the writer's desire (*yu* 欲) for *zhiji zhe* 知己者 , "one who recognizes the true self."[1]

It is here that we may recall the French phenomenologist Maurice Merleau-Ponty's statement on the perception of a work of art:

---

1. I am indebted to Martin W. Huang's discussion of this phase in *Desire and Fictional Narrative in Late Imperial China* (Cambridge, Mass.: Harvard University Asia Center, 2001), 76.

Plate 6. Fukushima Keidō, *Bright and Clear*, ink on paper, 13.5" x 53".
明歴々

The accomplished work is thus not the work which exists in itself like a thing, but the work which reaches its viewer and invites him to take up the gesture that created it and, skipping the intermediaries, to rejoin, without any guide other than a movement of the invented line (an almost incorporeal trace), the silent world of the painter, henceforth uttered and accessible.[2]

In this essay we will examine the distinctive way *zhiji*, "recognition of the true self," manifests itself within a particular genre of calligraphy known in Japan as *bokuseki* (Chinese: *moji* 墨跡. *Bokuskei* (literally, "traces of ink") was a term used during the Muromachi period (1336–1573) by tea ceremony and Buddhist Masters, for original works by Chan 禪 (Japanese: Zen) Buddhist monks. It also included the writings of lay Chinese scholars considered to have been influenced by their association with Chan monks. The term "old *bokuseki*" was reserved for Chan calligraphy from the Song (960–1279) and Yuan (1260–1368) Dynasties, and is a reflection of the respect accorded these early works in later Japan.

Our examination will center on two late Northern Song calligraphic inscriptions, Yuanwu Keqin's (1063–1135) *Certificate of a Disciple's Awakening* (*Yinke zhuang*), in the Tokyo National Museum (**Figure 1, p. 42**), and Huang Tingjian's (1045–1105) *Li Taibo's "Recalling Past Wanderings" Poem Scroll* (*Li Taibo Yijiuyu Shijuan*), in the Fujii Museum, Tokyo (**Figure 3, p. 46**). These works will be shown to have served as the exemplary precedents upon which the cultural authority of *bokuseki* is derived. Through an examination of these works we intend to shed light on the importance of calligraphy as a contemplative aesthetic practice for a school of Buddhism that is predicated on achievement of enlightenment "not dependent on words."[3]

---

2. Maurice Merleau-Ponty, "Indirect Languages and the Voices of Silence," in *Signs*, trans. Richard C. McCleary (Evanston: Northwestern University Press, 1964), 51.

3. For a succinct discussion of the legendary origins of Chan Buddhism, see Helmut Brinker and Hiroshi Kanazawa, *Zen Masters of Meditation in Images and Writings* (Zurich: Artibus Asiae Publishers, Supplementum 40, 1996), 25.

Plate 7. Fukushima Keidō, *Appear with Dignity*, ink on paper, 13.5" x 53".

露度々

The Primacy of Gesture

Preparatory to a discussion of our topic, I wish to present a partial epistemography of Chinese calligraphy; in other words, to address what it is that we must attend to when discussing a calligraphic work of art. This will engage us in a phenomenological description of the perceptual experience of calligraphy made concrete as an aesthetic object, that takes the form of a radical reflection upon a calligraphic inscription's mode of *presentation*—its visual nature—to the viewing subject. It is a consideration of the perceptual experience that presupposes a conception of the perceived aesthetic-*object* and the perceiving viewing-*subject* as they appear within the experiential space of aesthetic encounter. Calligraphy as given in perception, that is as percept, is locatable neither simply subjectively in the mind's eye of the viewing subject (i.e., as an ideational or cognitive construct) nor objectively in the material work of art (i.e., as an empirical or sensible datum).

In its visual nature, calligraphy makes manifest the *primacy of gesture* in both its production and aesthetic reception. Discernible in the "traces of ink" are references back to the originary intertwining of three fundamental sensory modalities: vision, motility, and touch. This sensory intertwining is precisely that which Merleau-Ponty has shown grounds us in the lived world. As Helen Fielding recently observed:

> Vision is not just visual signification but is also bodily experience intrinsically tied to touch and to motility. Indeed, we only understand what we see as subjects who move in and engage with the world; the eye itself moves as the object of vision shifts.[4]

---

4. Helen Fielding, "Envisioning the Other: Lacan and Merleau-Ponty on Intersubjectivity," in *Merleau-Ponty, Intersubjectivity and Exteriority, Physical Life and the World,* ed. Dorothea Olkowski and James Morely (Albany: State University of New York Press, 1999), 191.

Plate 8. Fukushima Keidō, *Everywhere and Everytime Become a Master,* ink on paper, 13.5" x 53".

隨處作主

Written characters thus root themselves securely in the senses and the world. And the world, for the Chinese, thus becomes a vast field of signs, of calligraphy.

A calligraphic inscription unfolds sequentially as characters are traditionally written down on a surface in vertical columns and aligned across in horizontal rows from right to left or left to right. An implied vertical axis at the center of each column serves as a coherence-generating constraint for the spatio-temporal structuring of the individual written characters. Our perception of the structure or formal organization they manifest continuously shifts both temporally and spatially as new elements are added from one stroke to the next, and from one character to the next. Time, to paraphrase Mikhail Bakhtin, takes on flesh, becomes visible through the material traces of the brush; likewise space becomes charged and responsive to the movements of time and the unfolding of the text. Calligraphy thus mobilizes a variety of complicated perceptual operations that impart to an inscription a distinct formal organization and communicative orientation or intent—legibility and coherence that is both intelligible and sensible. This is often dependent on the genre expectations of the particular calligraphic script (e.g., *cao shu* 草書, or cursive script) and mode of literary text (e.g., *tie* 帖, or informal letter). The perception of visual coherence is manifest in the specific spatio-temporal structuring of the character formations. And this is engendered by the particular pattern of spatial arrangement and temporal rhythms associated with the originary intertwining of the three fundamental sensory modalities noted above: vision, motility, and touch. In their interleaving, they impart to calligraphy its dynamic of configurational forces (*shi* 勢) and spatio-temporal coherence.

The tactility and motility disclosed within the visual nature of the ink traces of the brush are indices of the formative process of their execution (i.e., signs relying on specific configurations of the body and the senses). In the production and reception of a calligraphic text:

- *Vision* comes into play in the spatial arrangement of character configurations and is experienced in the particular patterning of dynamic stability and balance assured by adherence to the vertical axis implied at the center of each column.

Plate 9. Fukushima Keidō, *Vast Emptiness, Nothing Sacred*, ink on paper, 13.5" x 53".

廓然無聖

- *Motility* finds expression through the movement of the brush, and is experienced in the trajectory, speed, and directional force of each brushstroke in its movements away from and back towards the central vertical axis of the character.

- *Touch* is registered in the angle of attack and accents of pressure and nuances of movement applied to the brush. It is experienced in terms of the relative thickness, weight, shape, and density of individual strokes, and as expansions and contractions in their contours with respect to an implied moving center internal to the strokes.

There is another sense of dynamic balance that assumes the individual nature of character configurations but not, however, in terms of axial stability and proportion. Usually associated with informal inscriptions written in running script (*xing shu* 行書) and cursive script, the balance of a character in this instance does not depend merely on its axial alignment, but on its dynamic center of motion. The dynamic center of motion is not pre-established like the implied vertical axis at the center of each column, but rather emerges spontaneously and intuitively through the rhythmic gestural movements of the brush in the execution of each character. This is perceptually experienced in the *huying* 呼應, or "responses" of the brushstrokes in their relations of visual interaction. The difference that arises between viewer expectations for character configurations exhibiting axial stability and rhythmic constancy (i.e., *pingzheng* 平正, or "balance and regularity"), on the one hand, and the aesthetic encounter of their "coherent deformation," on the other, can be thought of as a site where the character opens up to the movements of the heart-mind. It is precisely in this liminal space that "recognition of the true self" of the writer may occur in calligraphy associated with *bokuseki*.

Plate 10. Fukushima Keidō, *I Don't Know*, ink on paper, 13.5" x 53".

不職

"Plain Tranquility" and the Calligraphy of Yuanwu Keqin

The inscription of poetic verses and sermons was a common practice among Chan monks in the Song dynasty (960–1269).[5] As Qianshen Bai has observed, "In China, Buddhist monks often were well-versed in secular texts as well as scriptures, and many were accomplished calligraphers."[6] We can gain an appreciation of the importance of these texts from the following comment by Helmut Brinker and Hiroshi Kanazawa:

> Although, or maybe precisely because, Zen set narrow limits
> to pious text worship and instead emphasized immediate per-
> sonal transmission of fundamental Buddhist insights, i.e.,
> "transmission from mind to mind," *yixin chuanxin* (Japanese:
> *ishin denshin*), the "true trace" inherent in the written word of
> an experienced religious Master was bound to be even of
> greater importance to the follower.[7]

The earliest extant "true trace" is Yuanwu Keqin's *Certificate of a Disciple's Awakening* (**Figure 1, p. 42**). It is a sermon from *Instructions to Long Zhicang* (*Shi Long Zhicang*), written by Yuanwu Keqin in 1124, at the age of 62, during his residence at the Tianningwanshou Monastery in Kaifeng, the capital of the Northern Song.

Yuanwu Keqin (1063–1135) was a disciple of Wuzu Fayin of the Yangqi sect of Linji (Japanese: Rinzai) school of Chan Buddhism. He is best known for his famous ten-volume *Blue Cliff Record*, a classic of Chan Buddhism, compiled toward the end of the Northern Song

---

5. For a comprehensive list of written documents that beside their literal content functioned as a means of spiritual communication, vide Helmut Brinker and Hiroshi Kanazawa, 101–2.

6. For a general discussion of this work, vide Qianshen Bai's entry in *The Embodied Image: Chinese Calligraphy from the John B. Elliott Collection* (Princeton: The Art Museum, Princeton University, 1999), 140.

7. Brinker and Kanazawa, 101.

Plate 11. Fukushima Keidō, *Go Have Some Tea*, ink on paper, 13.5" x 53".

喫茶去

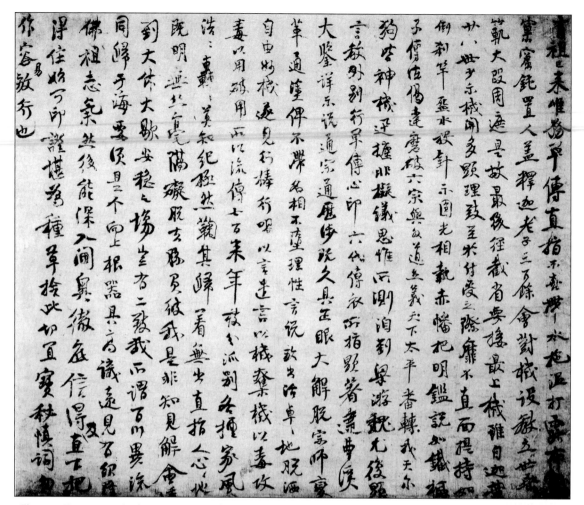

Figure 1. Yuanwu Keqin (*1063–1135*), *Certificate of a Disciple's Awakening (Yinke zhuang)*, Tokyo National Museum.

while he was residing at the Lingqian Hall in Hunan Province. For this he was granted the title *Foguo* ("Enlightened One") by Emperor Huizong. With the fall of Kaifeng to invading Jin armies, he fled southward and took up residence in the Jinshan Monastery, where Emperor Gaozong granted him the name Yuanwu.

Texts such as Yuanwu Keqin's *Certificate of a Disciple's Awakening* "had the function—besides their literal content—of allowing a spiritual communication with the writer beyond all spatial-temporal dimensions."[8] Inscribed in *xing-kai* 行楷, or "running standard" script,

---

8 *Ibid.*

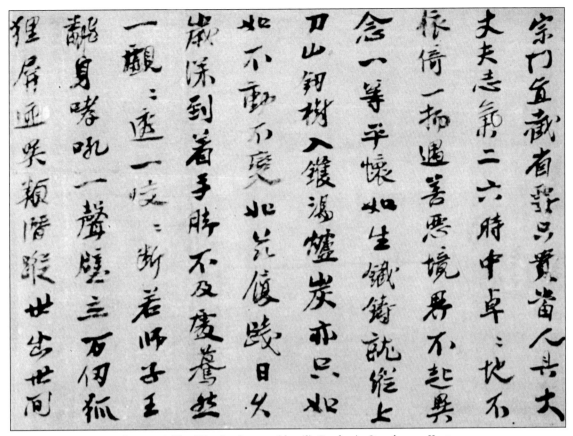

Figure 2. Mi'an Xianjie, *Sermon* (detail), Ryuko-in Storehouse, Kyoto.

Certificate of a Disciple's Awakening realizes a "naturalness" of execution referred to in the aesthetic writings of the day as *ziran* 自然 ("spontaneity," "naturalness," and "self-doing") and *tianzhen*天眞 (literally, "heavenly or natural perfection"). These terms refer to qualities of brushwork indicative of a naturalness of the person, untethered by a self-consciousness of style and intent. These aesthetic ideals were of paramount concern in aesthetic theories and practices of writing among scholars in the late Northern Song.9

The term that best captures the specific quality of expression in Yuanwu Keqin's *Certificate of a Disciple's Awakening*, however, is *pingdan* 平淡 ("plain tranquility," or

9. For a discussion of this issue in the aesthetic theory and calligraphy of Mi Fu (1052–1107/8) and the scholar-officials of the late Northern Song, see Peter Sturman, *Mi Fu: Style and the Art of Calligraphy in Northern Song China* (New Haven and London: Yale University Press, 1997), 150–72; and Susan Bush, *The Chinese Literati on Painting from Su Shih (1037–1101) to Tung Ch'i-ch'ang (1555–1636)*, Harvard-Yenching Institute Studies 27, 2nd ed. (Cambridge, Mass: Harvard University Press, 1978), 72.

"simplicity with underlying depth").[10] This term refers to the profundity of spirit that lies beneath the seeming simplicity at the surface of the text. Peter Sturman notes that "as an attribute *pingdan* becomes manifest not *in* a style but in one's approach to giving shape to style. In this regard, *pingdan* becomes practically interchangeable with the concept of naturalness: what emerges without reflection from a state of equilibrium."[11] *Pingdan,* as realized in the calligraphy of Yuanwu Keqin, elicits from the viewer "recognition of the true self" (*zhiji*) of the writer as one who has attained equanimity and quiescence of spirit.

The transmission of *pingdan* as an aesthetic ideal can be seen in subsequent sermons written by Chan monks. A fine example is that of Mi'an Xianjie, in the Ryuko-in Storehouse, Kyoto (**Figure 2, p. 43**). Mi'an Xianjie was a monk in the lineage of Yuanwu Keqin. He wrote this sermon at Wanshou Monastery, in August 1179, in response to a request by the Chan Practitioner Zhang. Inscribed when the Master was sixty-two, it can be taken as a *shenhui* 神會, or "communion of the spirit" with the earlier Master, Yuanwu Keqin. Numbered among Mi'an Xianjie's many students,

> Songyuan Chongyue (1132–1202), Caoyuan Daosheng, and Poan Zuxian (1136–1211) each founded their own schools, which were transmitted to Japan and were the source of the twenty-four schools of Zen that arose there. In other words, Xianjie is the patriarch of all of these schools, and as a result, this work is valued very highly by Zen and tea ceremony schools and their followers in Japan. [12]

---

10. *Pingdan* was originally a Daoist concept and first appears in the *Daodejing* and *Zhuangzi*. For a discussion, vide Sturman, 139.

11. *Ibid.,* 153.

12. Yujiro Nakata. *Chinese Calligraphy* (New York, Tokyo, Kyoto: Weatherhill/Tankosha, 1983), 196.

Plate 12. Fukushima Keidō, *Every Day Is a Good Day*, ink on paper, 13.5" x 53".

日々是好日

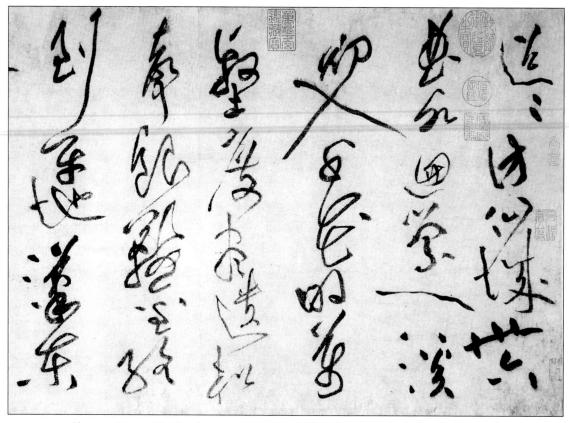

Figure 3. Huang Tingjian (1045–1105), *Li Taibo's "Recalling Past Wanderings" Poem Scroll
(Li Taibo Yijiuyu Shijuan)*, detail, Fujii Museum, Tokyo.

The Spontaneous Unconventionality of Huang Tingjian

A second important artistic lineage of *bokuseki* is represented by the calligraphy of a contemporary of Yuanwu Keqin, the poet-calligrapher Huang Tingjian (1045–1105). Huang was
one of a number of literati who showed great interest in Chan Buddhism during the Song
period. Brinker and Kanazawa note that Huang Tingjian

> often used in his writings Buddhist terminology unmistakably
> influenced by Chan thought. This is not surprising since he
> was close to several Masters of meditation, among them the
> painter-monk Huaguang Zhongren (died 1123) celebrated for
> his monochrome ink paintings of plum blossoms. Thus

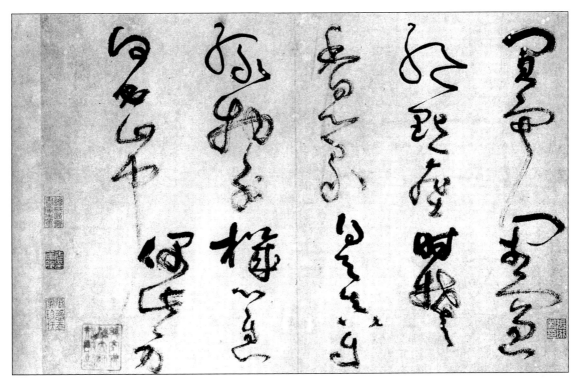

Figure 4. Zhina (1078–1157), *Poem in Cursive Script*, The John B. Elliott Collection,
The Art Museum, Princeton University.

Huang's *Collected Works* contain the following passage: "I used
to say of writing that brushwork in character is like insight in
the sayings of the Chan Masters." [13]

Brinker and Kanazawa go on to comment that "by this Huang Tingjian meant that in
order to penetrate the spirit and the essence of the art of writing, neither indefatigable study
nor zealous exercise and coping were of any help; only intuitive empathy, attained in a flash-
like moment of enlightenment, could reveal the substance of the work." [14]

At a time when it was common practice to follow in the classical tradition of the calligraphy of Wang Xizhi (303–361), Huang Tingjian sought in his writings a spontaneous and
untrammeled expression, one which was not the outcome of a preconceived idea or mediating

---

13. Brinker and Kanazawa, 100.
14. *Ibid.*

corpus of conventional brushstrokes.[15] This is exemplified in Huang Tingjian's *Li Taibo's "Recalling Past Wanderings" Poem Scroll* (**Figure 3, p. 46**). Completed in 1094, it is an inscription of a poem by the T'ang poet Li Bo "recalling his old travels, presented to General Yuan San of Qiao District."[16]

In this work, Huang employs several brush techniques, such as the "double-hook, suspended wrist and arm" technique (*shuanggou xuanwan* 雙鉤懸腕), that enabled him to effectively generate internal energies that were directed and released in the form of "brush force or momentum" (*bishi* 筆勢), through the movements of the arm and shoulder forming a single continuous unit with the brush. The "double-hook" refers to the shape of the fore and middle fingers as they press against the brush and the fourth finger.[17] It is through such techniques that Huang Tingjian set up the conditions for "seizing" or "withholding and releasing" (*qinzong* 禽縱) energy that enabled him to achieve what he termed *chenzhuo tongkuai* 沈著痛快 ("weighty intensity with a satisfying ease").[18] Mi Fu (1051–1107) referred to this as "self-soing naturalness" (*ziran tianzhen* 自然天眞), a creative process that results in a selfless expression of one's "original nature" unencumbered by either personal or societal intent.[19]

In *Li Taibo's "Recalling Past Wanderings" Poem Scroll*, the inattention to axial alignment and the seeming awkwardness or ungainliness of the character configurations, referred to in Chinese as *zhuo* 拙, are precisely the marks of an immediacy and naturalness that would have appealed to Chan Buddhist monks; such expression transcended the conventional duality of aesthetic beauty and ugliness. To quote, once again, Brinker and Kanazawa: "The declared

---

15. For a discussion of the classical tradition, vide Lothar Ledderose, *Mi Fu and the Classical Tradition of Chinese Calligraphy* (Princeton: Princeton University Press, 1979).

16. Yujiro Nakata, 188.

17. For an extensive discussion of the brush methods of Huang Tingjian, vide Fu Shen C. Y. "Huang T'ing-chien's Calligraphy and His *Scroll for Chang Ta-t'ung*: A Masterpiece Written in Exile," Ph.D. diss., Princeton University, 1976, 106–18.

18. *Ibid.,* 108.

19. Sturman, 171.

Plate 13. Fukushima Keidō, *The Oak Tree in Front of the Garden*, ink on paper, 13.5" x 53".

庭前柏樹子

庶為梅傳子

ambition of Zen Masters was to give visible expression to their own true self, following the example of independent literati and aspiring to the ideal of their creed."[20]

The immediate influence that Huang Tingjian's calligraphy would have on Chan monks can be seen in *Poem in Cursive Script*, composed and inscribed by Zhina (1078–1157), in the John B. Elliott Collection at Princeton's Art Museum (**Figure 4, page 47**). Zhina was a Chan monk who served as Abbot of the Lingyin Temple in Hangzhou, capital of China during the Southern Song period. The poem is an autobiographical reflection on a Chan Buddhist theme:

> Peaceful, silent, my window is dustless;
>
> Sometimes, burning incense, I attain naturalness.
>
> Transcending the material world,
>
> I leave behind worldly concerns—
>
> No need to retreat to the mountains.[21]

As noted previously, the "dustless" window makes reference to the "dust of the world," a Buddhist metaphor for spiritual ignorance, that which clouds the mind and entraps one in a dualistic, subject-object experience of separation from the world.[22] The sentiment expressed in the poem, the attainment of a state of "naturalness," of unmediated engagement with the world, is visually expressed in the brushwork that, following the precedent of Huang Tingjian, is propelled by "configurational forces" (*shi* 勢) unencumbered by conventional constraints. The characters or connected-character sequences do not strictly adhere to the implied vertical axis at the center of each row, veering or drifting to either side or shifting diagonally upward or downward to the left. The "energy-momentum" (*qishi* 氣勢) generated in the ink-saturated initial strokes continues uninterrupted in the inscription of the lines of the poem until the ink runs dry. These techniques represent an attempt to realize an expression of naturalness— indicative of a naturalness of the person—"to give visible expression to one's own true self."

---

20. Brinker and Kanazawa, 100.

21. Translated by Qianshen Bai, *Embodied Image*, 180.

22. This description is derived from my discussion in which I argue that the poem was indebted to the calligraphy of Huang Tingjian. Vide Stephen J. Goldberg, "Tradition and Authorial Identity in Chinese Calligraphy: Three Works from the Elliott Collection," in *Oriental Art* XLVI, no. 5 (2000): 31.

Bokuseki Calligraphy as a Contemplative-Aesthetic Practice

This brings us finally to a discussion of the role of calligraphy as a contemplative aesthetic practice within Chan Buddhism. Chan (literally, "meditation") is a sect of Buddhism first introduced into China around 500 C.E. by the Indian monk Bodhidharma (Chinese: Puti Damo, Japanese: Bodai Daruma, died before 534). It differed significantly from other schools of Buddhism that were dependent on textual and doctrinal interpretation, by advocating a more direct approach to the attainment of enlightenment not dependent on words.

In Chan Buddhism one relies on "one's own power" (Chinese: *zili* 自力; Japanese: *jiriki*) as opposed to "another's power" (Chinese: *tali* 他力; Japanese: *tariki*), be it a priest, sutra, or Buddhist image. The path to enlightenment traditionally takes the form of two fundamental practices: *zazen* 坐禪 (Chinese: *zuochan*), or "sitting in meditation," and the *kōan* (Chinese: *gong'an* 公安), a "paradoxical utterance . . . used as a meditative focus for Zen training."[23] The *kōan*, given by the Master to the disciple for contemplation, was a linguistic construct designed to frustrate the "habits of the heart" in framing one's experiences of self and world in dualistic, subject-object dichotomies. Its contemplation was intended to bring one, in time, to the point of utterly exhausting the preconceived categories of rational thought typically relied upon in taking up the world. Then, as a result of the persistent meditation and contemplation of the *kōan*, a simple action and accompanying sound, such as that of the sweeping of leaves within the walls of a temple courtyard, could precipitate, quite suddenly, the moment of enlightenment, known in Japanese as *satori*. It is here, in the unassuming and non-spectacular phenomenal world of nature, that one may attain a fleeting glance of the "not-yet-articulated" or "pre-phenomenal reality" (Chinese: *wu* 無; Japanese: *mu*, or "nothingness"), which lies beyond human phenomenal or existential reality (Chinese: *you* 有; Japanese: *yu*, or "being").

This concept is expressed in the following anecdote: "A monk once asked Master Jōshū (Chinese: Chao-chou), 'Has a dog the Buddha nature or not?' Jōshū said, '*Mu!*'"[24] According to Thomas Kasulis:

---

23. T. P. Kasulis, *Zen Action, Zen Person* (Honolulu: University of Hawai'i Press, 1985), 10.
24. *Ibid.*

Jōshū eluded the trap in the monk's question by refusing to be
caught in the relative viewpoints affirming or denying the
presence of Buddha-nature in the dog. In this respect, his
"Mu!" is not "No!" addressed to the question asked. Rather, it
is a refusal to accept the conceptual distinctions which give
the question meaning.[25]

As Shin'ichi Hisamatsu observes, "When the meaning of *mu* is realized truly, the true self,
the formless self, is awakened. In other words, far from simply meaning 'no,' *mu* is Zen itself.
The true and living self, the self in the Zen sense, is *mu*." He goes on to identify Chao-chou's
mu with the character *mu* inscribed by Hakuin Ekaku (1686–1769; **Figure 5, opposite page**).
"Thus when Hakuin wrote this character he attempted to depict this self. He was writing *mu*
not in its usual sense but Chao-chou's *mu*. As Chao-chou's *mu* assumes written form, it is
Chao-chou's *mu* that is writing. *Mu* writes *mu*."[26] It is in this state of "undifferentiatedness,"
in which "it could be said that Hakuin himself took the form of this character *mu* and therein
manifested himself,"[27] that one comes to understand what is meant by the phrase "Zen action
Zen person."

Likewise, each of the calligraphic works we have identified as *bokuseki* is marked by a
refusal to accept the conceptual distinctions between aesthetic beauty and ugliness or, for that
matter, between calligraphy and non-calligraphy. Rather than be constrained by the norms
and conventions of traditional calligraphic practice, the calligrapher sought a spontaneity and
naturalness of execution that elicits from the viewer *zhiji*, or "recognition of the true self."

Commenting on the seeming contradiction in the Zen attitude toward calligraphy and
language, Fukushima Keidō Rōshi explains:

It is not simply a negation of words and letters. Rather, what
is being negated is the attachment to the word. This is because

---

25. *Ibid.*, 13.
26. Shin'ichi Hisamatsu, *Zen and the Fine Arts,* trans. Gishin Tokiwa (Tokyo: Kodansha International, Ltd., 1971), 67.
27. *Ibid.*, 67–8.

words and letters both consist of something having to do with intellectual knowledge, so to transcend words implies the transcendence of knowledge. So to not rely on words means to not be attached to words; it does not mean to not use them or negate them. On the contrary, it means that you can truly, freely use them.[28]

Figure 5. Hakuin Ekaku (1686–1769), the character *mu.*

I shall now conclude with what is truly an exemplary expression of Zen use of words, Liang Kai's (active first half of the thirteenth century) *Li Bo Chanting a Poem with the Moon*, in the Tokyo National Museum (**Figure 6, p. 54**). The T'ang poet is here portrayed looking upward with lips pursed and eyes totally focused on that which is not made present, the mid-autumn moon. Rather than turning away to compose a poem with the subjective experience of the moon as its object, Li Bo stays engaged with the moon and begins to chant. And thus, the chanted poem is neither a subjective expression of his inner feelings, nor is it an objectification of the moon. Rather, in this contemplative-aesthetic moment of subject-object encounter, the experience of undifferentiatedness is allowed to *form itself* in his words.

Likewise, in the immediacy and spontaneity of the calligraphic brushwork employed in rendering the T'ang poet, we recognize an indexical sign and inscription of Liang Kai's originary gestures in the visible traces of ink. In its existentiating function, the brushstroke opens up a difference that articulates the surface into figural subject and the surrounding world

---

28. Fukushima Keidō, from his guest lecture for the "Beyond Words" seminar, University of Richmond, spring 1994. Quoted in Audrey Yoshiko Seo and Stephen Addiss, *The Art of Twentieth-Century Zen: Paintings and Calligraphies by Japanese Masters* (Boston: Shambala, 1998), 14.

Figure 6. Liang Kai (active first half 13th century), *Li Bo Chanting a Poem with the Moon*, Tokyo National Museum.

of the work. Characteristic of the Chan, or Zen, contemplative aesthetic, it captures that liminal region between the phenomenal, or articulated world (Japanese: *yu* 有) and pre-phenomenal, or not-yet-articulated world (Japanese: *mu* 無). It is here that we experience in the soft, silvery traces of unsaturated ink the gradual dissolving or devolving of the subject back into the ground of the surface, the undifferentiated surrounding blank surface, which the Japanese term *yo-haku*. It is this experience that the Japanese Buddhist monk Saigyō (1118–1190) so beautifully expressed in the following poem:

> A man whose mind is
>
> At one with the sky-void steps
>
> Inside a spring mist
>
> And thinks to himself he might
>
> In fact step right out of the world.[29]

We began our discussion with an inquiry into precisely how recognition (*zhi*)—the basic relation we have with others and the world—functions in a distinctive way within calligraphy. As we have seen, in calligraphic inscriptions associated with *bokuseki*, the elicitation of "recognition of the true self" was predicated on an explicit departure from the classical tradition of calligraphic practice. The question of expression and recognition in *bokuseki* as a signifying practice is thus deeply implicated in identities and sources of authority and their contestation. This is to advocate for a notion of recognition as "acknowledgement or affirmation"[30] that is mediated by relations of cultural authority. In traditional China, cultural authority is always derived from allusion within one's own aesthetic practice to exemplary precedents. In this respect, we come to appreciate how Yuanwu Keqin and Huang Tingjian served as sources of cultural authority for two very important artistic lineages of *bokuseki* calligraphy.

---

29. Translated by William R. Lafleur in "Saigyō and the Buddhist Value of Nature," in *Nature in Asian Traditions of Thought: Essays in Environmental Philosophy,* ed. J. Baird Callicott and Roger T. Ames (Albany: State University of New York Press, 1989), 202.

30. Webb Keane, *Signs of Recognition: Powers and Hazards of Representation in an Indonesian Society* (Berkeley: University of California Press, 1997), 15.

Bokki and *Zen No Sho*

APPROACHING THE WORK OF FUKUSHIMA KEIDŌ RŌSHI

Jason M. Wirth

In calligraphy there is usually a form or formality to be followed; in this it is no different from realism. But this is not true of Zen calligraphy, which is never bound by the preestablished forms of letters. The unconstrained facility of Zen springs from this freedom. It matters not the least whether the characters are distorted or not. And yet, by having the Formless Self as its base, what is thus written somehow keeps an orderly arrangement. Since the arrangement comes from this base, it springs forth unintentionally. When one goes on writing without thinking of doing this or that, the spacing of the characters will be orderly. When one holds the brush poised over the paper, there, already, space is established as one's Self, that is, as the space of Nothingness. Then,

Plate 14. Fukushima Keidō, *Watch Your Step!*, ink on paper, 13.5" x 53".

照顧脚下

when the characters appear, because of the space of Nothingness, they spring forth clearly, with characteristics different from those of ordinary characters.

—Hisamatsu Shin'ichi[1]

When you know everything, you are like a dark sky.
Sometimes a flashing will come through the dark sky.

—Suzuki Shunryū, *Zen Mind, Beginner's Mind*

Some calligraphers are able to do calligraphy like the natural flowing of water. That is how Zen Masters strive to do it.

—Fukushima Keidō Rōshi

What is Zen Calligraphy?

In approaching one of Fukushima's Zen calligraphies, one might ask what gives them their Zen character? What makes them works of Zen calligraphy as opposed to straightforward calligraphic inscriptions?

That they are by a Zen Master would be an insufficient answer because it says little about what makes this fact decisive. Simply to say that Zen calligraphy is as such because it was inscribed by a Zen Master tells us little about what is characteristic of this inscription process. It sounds more like an aside or a curious feature of the work.

Yet to say that a work of Zen calligraphy is as such because it deals with a Zen theme is no less vague. It is true that Fukushima's calligraphy employs sayings from Zen's rich history of poetry

---

1. Hisamatsu, *Zen and the Fine Arts*, trans. Gishin Tokiwa (Tokyo: Kodansha International, 1971), 73. Henceforth ZFA. This is a superb monograph.

Plate 15. Fukushima Keidō, *Old Pines Speak Wisdom, Hidden Birds Whisper Truth*, ink on paper, 13.5" x 53".
古松談般若幽鳥弄真如

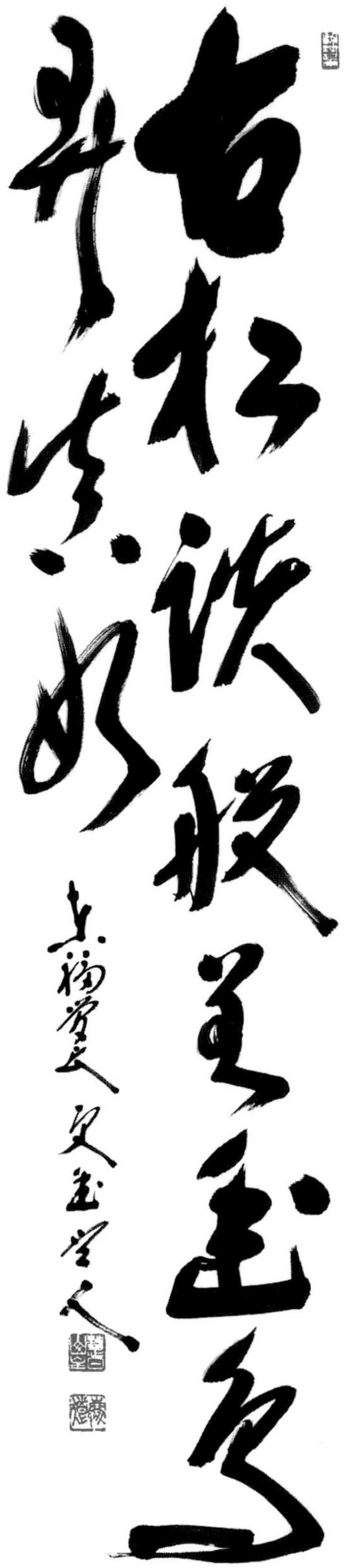
古松談般若
幽鳥弄真如

and *Goroku* ("*Records*") of the sayings and doings of past Zen Masters. It does not follow, how-ever, that every time a calligrapher, no matter how technically accomplished, inscribes a Zen say-ing that it is Zen calligraphy. It is critical that such an inscription emerge from Zen experience.

In this sense, a work of Zen calligraphy is irreducible to either its technical accomplish-ments (i.e., its competence within the norms of traditional calligraphic practice) or its literal message. It is true that the Zen saying is being presented as an important doctrine and, as such, partially for pedagogical reasons. Yet the calligraphy is not a fancy or ornate presenta-tion of a concept or an ideological position, nor is the emphasis of the work simply the com-munication of an idea.

What then is communicated in a work of Zen calligraphy when it is irreducible to either its formal or conceptual aspects? As Fukushima explained in an interview found elsewhere in this book, "The main point of both Zen and Zen calligraphy is Zen mind." Zen calligraphy emerges from the depths of Zen experience and it is an *expression*—not representation—of *mushin*. Zen calligraphy is therefore primarily neither the articulation nor the illustration of an idea.

Yet how is this *mushin* expressed, and how is it detected in the act of appreciating a work of Zen calligraphy? This question shall form the substance of this essay. In adopting this ques-tion as my leitmotif, I acknowledge from the outset the limitations of my approach. Employing philosophic and aesthetic descriptive ideas does not supplant the priority of developing one's own fundamental practice. As we shall see, Zen mind cannot be directly communicated. It is rather a question of beginning to cultivate one's own Zen experience, which emerges from one's own fundamental practice, and then of gaining entrance, even as a viewer, into the realm of what some call *hitsuzendō*, the *dao* of the Zen brush (*hitsu* = "brush"). Yet Zen mind cannot be isolated to any particular act. Rather, Zen calligraphy fol-lows from a Zen mind that animates all aspects of one's life, and hence one might say that it is the *dao* of the Zen mind, *mushin*, that freely animates the brush.

Zenki

How does *mushin* express itself in the case of Zen calligraphy? On the one hand, it does so with great freedom and individuality. If one looks at the history of *Zen no sho* (Zen calligra-phy), one finds a striking variety of styles, almost as if Zen calligraphy expressed *mushin* in unique ways, forming the record of something like that person's unique Zen personality. Yet it does not follow that one can consciously decide to start cultivating and expressing a Zen personality, much in the same way that many Americans are obsessed with finding themselves and expressing their individuality again and again, even holding the world hostage to the demands of their personality. Such self-expression is born of the ego and is predicated on the discovery and promotion of one's substantial self. In the cultivation of this self, one might endeavor to improve oneself and acquire new skills that enhance the attractiveness of the ego. In so doing, one might take up calligraphy as part of one's arsenal of tools for the great monologue of self-expression. Calligraphy becomes a means to an end, and it becomes a self-conscious activity. Perhaps wanting to appear like a great Zen Master, one might imitate Hakuin's "broken" style or even the gentle yet tremulous force of Fukushima's style.

Yet Zen calligraphy does not emerge from imitating externally the styles of those with whom one wishes to associate one's ego as it jostles for better position and recognition. Zen calligraphy, in emerging from *mushin*, becomes possible in what the Mahāyāna tradition sometimes calls the "great death." It is the liberation of what Hisamatsu called the formless self from the shackles of the ego. In this way, Zen calligraphy is not self-expression in the traditional sense of giving expression to the ego and its feelings and thoughts. It emerges from the "great death" and is a non-self-conscious (there cannot be self-consciousness without an ego) and free expression of *mushin*.

In this sense, one could speak of Zen calligraphy as an expression of *zenki*, of Zen activity or Zen force.[2] It is the expression of one's Zen mind in activity. Yet the force and activity of this Zen mind is not the energy of something in particular, and in this sense it is the exact opposite of traditional ego-expression. *Mushin* is the vitality of *nothing*, and as such is the transcending of the pernicious fiction that one has a root ego and intrinsic personality.

In Zen, *ki* is not something for which one can consciously strive—for who would do this striving other than the ego? Rather, in one's fundamental practice one unblocks one's access to what the Mahāyāna tradition sometimes calls one's "original face." As Fukushima articulates it (in the interview following this essay):

---

2. Hisamatsu reminds us that *zenki* also has the connotations of "wellspring, movement, dynamism, impulse, thrust, spontaneity, immediacy" (ZFA, 11).

Professional calligraphers self-consciously try to cultivate this *ki*, but in the Zen Master it is just something that is there naturally and which naturally finds expression. Perhaps one difference between a Zen Master and a professional, technically competent calligrapher is that the Zen Master does one piece and it is naturally there. The technical calligrapher keeps writing the character as he tries to develop *ki*.

Paradoxically the transcendence of the ego and its pernicious fiction of inherent individuality expresses itself as *zenki* with dazzling and great individuality. Having no form, the self cannot be said to be one's intrinsic personality or one's immortal ego-soul. Yet the formless self constantly and freely comes into form in individual ways. The formless self is empty and hence cannot be thought of as a thing having essence, yet it expresses itself with a force greater than any substantial self.

The Zen expression of individuality, so to speak, has nothing to do with the obsessive narcissism of egoism. In the latter one is always trying to find oneself or express one's self. As such, one is perpetually in a kind of Hobbesian war of all against all as egos clash with each other and jostle for position. In Zen, on the other hand, individuality is an expression of the utter non-individuality and nothingness of one's "original face" or what the great ninth-century Zen Master Rinzai (Chinese: Lin-chi), the founder of the Zen sect of which Fukushima is a member, called "the true person of no rank." In the Zen tradition, the formless self is the "utterance before voice" and "prior to the separation of heaven and earth."3

The formless self has nothing to do with the traditional religious desire to save one's soul and to go to heaven or the Pure Land. As Fukushima is wont to say, "Only the ego wants to go to heaven or the Pure Land." Would the ego want to go to heaven if it could

3. Vide ZFA, 12–13.

Plate 16. Fukushima Keidō, *Scoop Water, the Moon Lies in Your Hands; Touch a Flower, the Fragrance Fills Your Robe*, ink on paper, 13.5" x 53".
掬水月在手弄花香満衣

掬水月在手
弄花香满衣

辛卯仲夏 文燕书于玉堂主人

Figure 1: Hakuin,
*Homage to Hell, the Great
Bodhisattva.*

not hold onto the fiction of its inherent personality and thus be present to the splendors of heaven? The desire to go to heaven is selfish and as such comes from a sensibility that Zen mind—and hence Zen calligraphy—transcends.

Yet even the great Rinzai reformer Hakuin (1686–1769)[4] lamented that he had begun Buddhist practice in an effort to avoid damnation. When Hakuin was young, his mother took him to a Nichiren (1222–1282) temple in Hara, where he learned of the horrors of hell. The priest spoke vividly of the Eight Scorching Hells and "He had every knee in the audience quaking, every liver in the house frozen stiff with fear. As little as I was, I was certainly no exception. My whole body shook in mortal terror."[5] Hakuin wanted *satori* because he did not want to go to one of the Eight Scorching Hells.

Hakuin later did a remarkable calligraphy that reads, "Homage to Hell, the Great *Bodhisattva*"[6] (**Figure 1, this page**). Why did Hakuin speak of hell as a force of compassion? On the one hand, it was the idea of hell that first drove Hakuin to meditate, although this motivation was itself born of the ego. Even though it was the ego that drove Hakuin to seek *satori*, it was a use of the ego in which the ego is eventually used against itself. The great Mādhyamika philosopher Śāntideva taught that one has to use the *kleśas* or defiled emotions against themselves. One has to be impatient in one's desire to cultivate patience. One has to be angry at anger and learn to hate hate. In so doing, one inaugurates a movement that overcomes its origin.

---

4. The reported dates for Hakuin's life vary greatly. I thank Jeff Shore for clarifying to me that such inconsistencies are chiefly due to the failure to distinguish lunar and solar calendars of the time. Hence, those who were born or died in the eleventh or twelfth month are placed in the wrong year. The classic *Zengaku Daijiten* ("*Great Dictionary of Zen Studies*") confuses this greatly. For further information on the correct dating of Hakuin's life, see Michel Mohr, "Hakuin," in *Buddhist Spirituality: Later China, Korea, Japan, and the Modern World*, ed. Y. Takeuchi, J. W. Heisig, P. L. Swanson, and J. S. O'Leary (New York: The Crossroad Publishing Company, 1999).

5. *Wild Ivy: The Spiritual Autobiography of Zen Master Hakuin*, trans. Norman Waddell (Boston: Shambhala, 1999), 9. Henceforth WI.

6. Vide WI, 11.

Hakuin's ego drove him to meditate, but meditation overcame the ego of the one who had originally sought the Pure Land of *satori*.

Fukushima recollects that he became a monk because he wanted to save nine generations of his family, a desire that one can acutely feel when one remembers that it was born of the grief of having just lost his older sister and his grandmother who had been like a mother to him. Yet in Zen experience, he came to see that one does not meditate for the benefit of oneself and one's own. One meditates for the benefit of the Other, for the sake of all sentient beings. As such, the ego puts into play in its very desire to save or improve itself through *zazen* (sitting meditation) a process that transcends and expunges the one who inaugurates it.

After the "great death," the *zenki* of Zen calligraphy is the expression of the formless self, of *mushin*. As such one is *kiai*, rife with *ki* ("energy"), and the application of ink in the free expression of Zen mind is *bokki*, ink that is rife with *ki*. In good Zen calligraphy, one can see the *bokki*, the *ki* in the ink, as an expression of the formless self.[7] *Bokki*, although it assumes that one has a strong competence in the calligraphic arts, transcends the duality of the technically or formally correct and the self-consciously errant and wild. *Bokki* is the manifestation of *zenki* in the ink. It is the capture of *ki* in the application of the ink itself, and the ink unselfconsciously appears vibrant, vital, confident, free, sometimes bold, but always overflowing with life. It is as if the ink, in having captured *ki*, in having become *bokki*, were now somehow animate. This is not done intentionally, for to search for *ki* is to lose *ki*. As Fukushima articulates it, "Good art comes from a pure mind. If someone wants self-consciously to do a painting just because they want to see it one day exhibited in the Tokyo National Museum, they are painting with a defiled mind."

Dharma Transmission

How does one see the formless self in calligraphic form? This question is inseparable from the problem of *dharma* transmission. It takes Zen mind to understand Zen mind and *zenki* and Zen calligraphy. Yet if one does not seek means to communicate *mushin* to those who have

---

7. For a short discussion of this, vide Ōmori Sōgen and Terayama Katsujō, *Zen and the Art of Calligraphy: The Essence of Sho*, trans. John Stevens (New York and London: Viking Penguin, 1990), 8–10.

not cultivated it, how can it be transmitted? How would one even know of it such that one would be motivated to seek it?

Fukushima alluded to this problem when he spoke of learning to appreciate his calligraphy or even Zen itself. "In the Zen tradition they speak of *dharma* transmission, and there is an expression that brings out what I am trying to say: 'Unless the mind of the disciple is in some way the same as the mind of the Master, the transmission cannot take place.' This is very much connected to art as well." Transmission requires *ishin denshin*, transmission "from mind (*shin*) to mind." In his superb *teishō* on the *Mumonkan* or *Gateless Barrier*, Fukushima's teacher, Shibayama Rōshi, reflected on the famous *kōan* on the problem of *dharma* transmission. When Śākyamuni Buddha was lecturing and he held up a flower, his disciple Kasho smiled. Śākyamuni knew that the *dharma* had been transmitted.[8] Shibayama called this "transmission of the untransmittable"[9] or what was once called "Buddha to Buddha testimony."[10]

In the same way that *satori* cannot be cultivated in the way that something is purchased at the mall, the transmission of *mushin*, even in the act of appreciating a work of Zen calligraphy, attends to the same paradox. As Fukushima said of his own work: "It is better, of course, that someone does have some Zen mind, and the closer it is to my mind, the more they will be able to appreciate the work." Furthermore, the problem of *dharma* transmission is not simply the problem of the communication barriers between Zen mind and a quotidian mind. It is also the question of communicating between depths of *kenshō*. The great Masters require a lifetime of fundamental practice and not just a moment of *satori* that somehow gives one a decoder card to all things Zen. As Fukushima said of the great Chan Master Jōshū: "I feel that in order for me to approach the mind of Jōshū, I need another ten or twenty years. If Jōshū were here now and he saw my calligraphy, he would probably say that it is not that good."

---

8. Shibayma Zenkei, *Zen Comments on the Mumonkan*, trans. Kudo Sumiko (New York: Harper and Row, 1974), 58. Henceforth ZC. After long being out of print, Shambhala has recently reprinted this invaluable text.

9. ZC, 60.

10. ZC, 62.

Plate 17. Fukushima Keidō, *Ensō: What Is This?*, ink on paper, 13.5" x 53".

円相是何麼

Emptiness

In the Mahāyāna tradition, the realization of *satori* is not only the "great death" of the becoming empty—beyond form and non-form—of the self,[11] it is the realization of the emptiness or *śūnyā-ta* of all beings. Beyond being and non-being, all things are interwoven and interdependent without out thereby distinctively and in isolation having their own being or self-nature (*svabhāva*). This is the Zen experience of the "dependent co-origination" or *pratītyasamutpāda* of all beings—their fullness in excess of their status of isolated logical entities. As Fukushima comments, "*Śūnyāta* does not mean that the world is empty of things. It is an emptiness that contains everything."

This emptiness as not a vacancy, but a fullness beyond the substance of things, is sometimes expressed in the *ensō* or Zen circle, which is elegant, vibrant, perfect, yet empty. It is its emptiness that allows a circle to be fully a circle. Its emptiness is the source of its fullness. As such, the *ensō* is a common expression of Zen mind, and Zen mind is not just the experience of the fullness of the self's own emptiness, but the emptiness of all things. It is as if the *ensō* inscribes itself as it emerges from itself and marks itself—and all things—as perfectly empty and emptily perfect. The *ensō* paints the *ensō* in the vital *zenki* born of the realization of *śūnyāta*.

In this way, the animation of the ink in *bokki* does not single out the ink as an especially vital location of *ki*. Since all things are holy, nothing in particular is holy. There is nothing sacred (**Plate 9, p. 37**). In the Mahāyāna tradition, it was not only the "heart-mind" (*shin* or *kokoro*)[12] that was empty, and it is not only the emptiness of the ink, bristling with vitality, that becomes a privileged vessel of *śūnyāta*. Rather these are a profound indication that all things are empty, that all things are devoid of inherent essence, and hence that all things are alive, flowing with *ki*, empty of the constipation of reification.

The life of things is a life beyond the duality of life and death. The latter suggests that things come into being and have their being and life until they lose it at death. Only when things are emptied of essence—and, as Nāgārjuna insisted, even emptiness must be emptied of

---

11. Hisamatsu's phrase the "formless self" captures this overcoming of the self as either something or the vacant absence of something. The nothing of the formless self is the empty self, having transcended both form and non-form. It is rather an aspect of the dependent co-origination (*pratītyasamutpāda*) and interrelationship without essence of all beings.

12. *Kokoro* or "heart-mind" indicates that the simple duality between heart and mind, affect and thought, body and mind, is, like all dualities, transcended.

itself—do they return to their original life. They return to their original life within, yet beyond, the apparent duality of life and death. It is the life of life, so to speak, the life that transcends life and death but which expresses itself as the animation and emptiness of all beings.

Creativity

If the expressivity of *mushin* is at the heart of Zen calligraphy and, indeed, at the heart of all *zenki*, all Zen activities, then it cannot be exclusively approached with concepts. This tends to be an underdeveloped consideration in many Western traditions, which not only stress the ego but the primacy of the intellect and habituation and training. As important as these things are—and they are critical—their root is *mushin*, and hence fundamental practice has to be at the heart of both intellectual and artistic endeavors. *Mushin* is the creative and free self-expression of the nothingness (beyond the duality of something and nothing) of the formless self.

Although this insight is largely underdeveloped in Western traditions, it is not altogether foreign to them. It is interesting to note that some modern Buddhist philosophers have found themselves sympathetic to thinkers like Friedrich Nietzsche (1844–1900), who, without being a Buddhist or having much respect for what little he knew of Buddhism, made some of the same discoveries. He disparagingly called the decadent or passive form of nihilism emerging in the wake of the Death of God "European Buddhism." Nonetheless, Nietzsche's own thinking has some important insights into what we have been calling the free and creative expressivity of *mushin*. As Nishitani Keiji claimed in his early study of nihilism (*Nihirizumu*, "*The Self-Overcoming of Nihilism*"): "Even though there may be in Nietzsche a radical misunderstanding of the spirit of Buddhism, the fact that he considered it in relation to nihilism shows how well attuned he was to the real issue."[13]

In his posthumously published autobiography of sorts, *Ecce Homo* (completed in 1888), Nietzsche wrote of a creative inspiration that transcends the agency of the ego and

---

13. Nishitani Keiji, *The Self-Overcoming of Nihilism*, trans. Graham Parkes and Setsuko Aihara (Albany: State University of New York Press, 1990), xxxiii. Nishitani goes on to claim that "Ironically, it was not in his nihilistic view of Buddhism but in such ideas as *amor fati* and the Dionysian as the overcoming of nihilism that Nietzsche came closest to Buddhism, especially to Mahāyāna." Vide *The Self-Overcoming of Nihilism*, 180.

instrumental and technical reason. In this respect, he strikingly does not take personal credit for having given birth to his magnum opus, *Thus Spoke Zarathustra*:

> Has anyone at the end of the nineteenth century a distinct conception of what poets of strong ages called *inspiration*? If not, I will describe it.—If one had the slightest residue of superstition left in one, one would hardly be able to set aside the idea that one is merely incarnation, merely mouthpiece, merely medium of overwhelming forces. The concept of revelation, in the sense that something suddenly, with unspeakable certainty and subtlety, becomes *visible*, audible, something that shakes and overturns one to the depths, simply describes the fact. One hears, one does not seek; one takes, one does not ask who gives; a thought flashes up like lightning [*wie ein Blitz leuchtet ein Gedanke auf*], with necessity, unfalteringly formed—I never had any choice.[14]

The imagination is ecstatic, standing outside of itself, no longer in possession of itself (as if it ever was), seeing, thinking, hearing as lightning, as light emerging—without why—from its dark precursor. This is not like a scene from *The Exorcist* in which one is possessed by an alien and demonic subject that subjugates one's own subjectivity. Rather, the activity of the imagination demonstrates that there never was an agent. In fact, the absence of an agent in the subject position is one of Nietzsche's continuing concerns throughout his writings. In *Twilight of the Idols* (1888), for example, Nietzsche argued that belief in human agency is one of the four great errors, namely, that of a false causality. "The 'inner world' is full of phantoms and false lights: the will is one of them. The will no longer moves anything, consequently no longer explains anything—it merely accompanies events, it can also be absent. The so-called 'motive': another error. Merely a surface phenomenon of consciousness, an

---

14. Friedrich Nietzsche, *Ecce Homo*, trans. R. J. Hollingdale (New York and London: Penguin, 1979), 72. I have made some minor emendations using the German edition, *Werke in drei Bänden*, volume two, edited by Karl Schlechta (Munich: Carl Hansler Verlag, 1955), 1131.

accompaniment to an act, which conceals rather than exposes the *antecedentia* of the act. And as for the ego! It has become a fable, a fiction, a play on words: it has totally ceased to think, to feel and to will!"[15]

The imagination is the non-dual reason of the body, its activity without agency: "your body and its great Reason: that does not say 'I' but does 'I.'"[16] Creation does not presuppose an agent who inaugurates and completes a creative act that results in a work of art. Such a presupposition is an example of one of the four great errors. Creation is rather the non-dual movement of the holistic body (the mind and body are inseparable and never fully distinct from one another) as, to use Nishida Kitarō's phrase, "activity without agency." Creation is not the unfolding of a matrix already at work. Technically it is not even a deed (i.e., something done by a doer). Nietzsche linked creativity with the lightning flash of the body that produces without subjectivity. No thing or no one is at work. Hisamatsu, one of Nishida's most prized students, called this "Awakening to the Self without Form," and he located this as central to Zen art: "that which is expressing itself and that which is expressed are identical"[17] and "that which paints is that which is painted."[18]

What seems new with Nietzsche already dramatically antedates Bodhidharma's *dharma* transmission to China in the sixth century C.E.[19] Already in the Daoist tradition there was an emphasis on meditation or what Zuangzi (Chuang Tzu) had called the "fasting of the mind." In a famous story in the *Zuangzi*, we learn of the mastery of Cook Ding, who, when he was butchering an ox for Lord Wen-hui with such precision and rhythm and prowess, was praised by the Lord. Ding sets down his knife and explains that it is not a question of skill, as if there were some technique to be mastered and then executed upon demand. "What I care about is *dao*, which goes beyond skill. When I first began cutting up oxen, all I could see was the ox itself. After three years I no longer saw the whole ox. And now—now I go at it by spirit and don't look with my eyes. Perception and understanding have come to a stop and spirit moves where it wants."[20]

---

15. *Götzen-Dämmerung, Twilight of the Idols*, trans. R. J. Hollingdale (New York and London: Penguin, 1990), 59.

16. "On the Despisers of the Body," *Also Sprach Zarathustra*, Schlechta, II, 300.

17. ZFA, 16.

18. ZFA, 19.

19. Although the legendary Bodhidharma is sometimes associated with the birth of Buddhism in China, Buddhism's arrival in China antedates Bodhidharma's arrival by several centuries.

20. This is from the third inner chapter of the *Zuangzi*. I am using Burton Watson's translation. *Chuang Tzu: Basic Writings* (New York: Columbia University Press, 1964), 46–47.

It is not that the *dao* simply gives Cook Ding a variety of epistemic perspectives by which to consider the best way to butcher the ox. When Cook Ding was just a hack, all he could see was the ox. The ox was before him. Of course, the ox could not be in front of him if he was not already first himself and, as such, was somebody who could be before something else. Skill always belongs to a more proficient hack because it is a technique belonging to someone, to a subject standing before an object. Cook Ding does not hack but rather cuts precisely because the ox is not before him and because there is no objective ox distinct from the butcher-agent. Rather, the cutting is the activity of spirit, which transcends the agency of the cutter. Cutting is an activity of *ki*, a part of a continuous movement between the abyssal formlessness of *dao* and the emerging into form of the activity of cutting. It is a continuous movement that combines opposites into a whole, namely, the formlessness of *dao* and the form of cutting. Indeed, Lord Wen-hui, by his own admission, learns from Cook Ding's analysis not just the secret of cutting, but the *dao* of life.

This is critical to Zen calligraphy. In Sun Qianli's T'ang Dynasty classic *Shu Pu* ("*Treatise on Calligraphy*," 687), he writes of this *dao* of calligraphy emerging in the transcending through mastery of the rules of calligraphy. "When one reaches complete mastery and the norms are clearly understood, the work will flow freely and easily; mental conception will come first and the brush will follow, casually and without effort; the ink will flow freely and the spirit will soar... Mastery is like Cook Ding's eyes, which need not see the whole ox."[21] In this sense one can speak of the creativity of Zen calligraphy as the *dao* (Japanese: *dō*) of calligraphy, or *shodō*.

The Sōtō Zen Master Suzuki Shunryū (1905–1971) compared the creativity of *mushin*, as did Nietzsche, to lightning flashing to the fore from nowhere. In the justly celebrated series of talks given at the end of his life and collected as *Zen Mind, Beginner's Mind*,[22] Suzuki Rōshi explained that Zen training acts to produce what he calls variously the "empty mind," or the "clear mind," or "no mind," or thinking as the "dark sky." "When you know everything, you are like a dark sky. Sometimes a flashing will come through the dark sky. After it passes, you forget all about it, and there is nothing left but the dark sky. The sky is never surprised when

---

21. *Two Chinese Treatises on Calligraphy*, trans. Chang Ch'ung-ho and Hans H. Frankel (New Haven: Yale University Press, 1995), 11.

22. Suzuki Shunryū, *Zen Mind, Beginner's Mind*, ed. Trudy Dixon (New York and Tokyo: Weatherhill, 1970). Henceforth ZM.

all of a sudden a thunderbolt breaks through. And when the lightning does flash, a wonderful sight may be seen. When we have emptiness we are always prepared for watching the flashing."[23] Hence Suzuki concluded that it "is absolutely necessary for everyone to believe in nothing. But I do not mean a voidness. There is something, but that something is something which is always prepared for taking some particular form, and it has some rules, or theory, or truth in its activity. . . . By enlightenment I mean believing in nothing, believing in something which has no form or color, which is ready to take form or color."[24] It is the non-dual nothing of the lightning body, always nothing becoming something.

Expressivity

I turn now to a consideration of the term *expressivity*, which I have been using rather than the term *representation*. The latter moves to recreate within the work an object that is outside the work. Expressivity is activity without agency, as *mushin* expresses and paints and inscribes itself from within itself. In a discussion with the German philosopher Martin Heidegger (died 1976) on *The Essence of the Arts* (May 18, 1958), Hisamatsu argued that:

> In the West, the source somehow exists as form; it is eidetic. In Zen, the root source is formless, nonbeing. But this 'non' is no mere negation. This nothingness is free of all form; formless, it can move and work freely and independently. This is the unhindered and independent movement out of which the work of art is produced.[25]

Heidegger found himself in sympathy with Hisamatsu, who further went on to claim that abstract painting is still bound to the duality of form and non-form. It is still bound to form in that it looks for "something beyond" form. Heidegger confessed that "our ideas of art fall

---

23. ZM, 84.

24. ZM, 118–19.

25. This conversation is collected in *Formless Self Awakening*, ed. Jeff Shore. This anthology unfortunately at this point remains unpublished. It originally appeared in *Listening to Heidegger and Hisamatsu*, ed. L. Alcopley (Kyoto: Bokubi Press, 1963).

short of the point which the Japanese have already reached," that is, they fall short of the transcendence of the duality of formal and abstract in Zen art. Fukushima made the same point about those who externally imitate the seemingly "broken" form of someone like Hakuin.

> Hakuin's Zen calligraphy is so great because not only has he developed his talent as a calligrapher, but also his Zen mind is perfectly expressed in his calligraphy. Hakuin's calligraphy is very unique. Yet it is important to understand that he is not just arbitrarily breaking with form. One has to understand the relationship between form and the unique breaking of form. I think that it is unfortunate that sometimes the Zen priests and the Zen Masters, without sufficient technical training, simply try to imitate Hakuin's free, broken style.

It is therefore not a question of either preserving or destroying form. In fact, it is not a question of consciously doing anything at all. Rather it is a question of the formless self, the original face, *coming into expression as the work of art.* It is, to borrow Hisamatsu's phrase, "the Fundamental Subject that is *Actively Nothing.*"[26]

Mushin, itself formless activity, expresses itself as form in Zen art and does so in such a way that the form captures its formless root within the form. It is an expression of formless activity. It is not a question of striving either to perfect form or to denigrate and annihilate form or to imagine that one can somehow represent the formless. Zen art *expresses* the vibrant non-representability of *mushin*. Hence Fukushima claimed that if two people were to set about inscribing an *enso*, and one was a monk with extensive Zen training and the other was just a kind of Zen tourist, the difference would be apparent. "The person without the Zen training would be intent on trying to make a perfect *enso* and in a sense be attached to that, and the Zen Master would be able to see that. The monk would be beyond that."[27]

---

26. ZFA, 51.
27. This is from the interview immediately following this essay.

Zen calligraphy then is an *expression* of *mushin* and, as such, has some things in common with elements of what came to be called Expressionism in the twentieth century. It is worth noting that some of the hard-won insights in modern art are already ancient insights in the Zen tradition. When one thinks of the vital strokes of a Franz Kline or a Robert Motherwell, one can already begin to detect some similarities. *Mushin* is "the fundamental subject" of expression, although it is not a proper subject in the Western sense. It is a formless, non-substantial activity in the subject position that expresses itself—without becoming the same—as the vitality of artistic objects. When Hisamatsu met with Paul and Hannah Tillich, the subject turned towards Hisamatsu's defense of the term *Expressionism*. Finding themselves sympathetic with Hisamatsu, the Tillichs brought up the example of Paul Klee as someone "expressive" in the Zen sense. Although Hisamatsu found himself sympathetic to the comparison, he was troubled by the agitated quality of Klee's abyss. "In Zen, darkness is an illuminating darkness. But the darkness in this painting is frightening. Zen darkness is calming."[28] Hisamtsu likened Klee's work to the fierce demons and tantric imagery of Shingon Buddhism. While that may be unfair to Klee—and even unfair to Shingon Buddhism—it is clear that Paul Klee's *oeuvre* is an important clue to an appreciation within a Western idiom of some aspects of the aesthetics inherent in Zen art. After all, Paul Klee in 1920 had argued:

> In the past artists represented things they had seen on earth, things they liked seeing or might have liked to see. Today they reveal the relativity of visible things; they express their belief that the visible is only an isolated aspect in relation to the universe as a whole, and that other, invisible truths are the overriding factors. Things appear to assume a broader and more diversified meaning, often seeming to contradict the rational experience of yesterday. The artist strives to express the essential character of the accidental.[29]

28. In *Formless Self Awakening*, 136.
29. Felix Klee, *Paul Klee*, trans. Richard and Clara Winston (New York: Georges Braziller, 1962), x.

Compassion and the *Bodhisattva* Way

Finally, it is important to remember that the expressivity of *zenki* as *mushin* that freely gives form to itself is not to be confused with a metaphysical position. It is the free experience of compassion or love. In the Mahāyāna tradition, emphasis is placed on both wisdom (*prajñā*) training and compassion (*karunā*) training. The Bodhisattvas, for example, were said to surrender their *satori* and emancipation from the cycles of birth and rebirth (*samsāra*) in order to love all sentient beings, endeavoring to eliminate their suffering. Yet it would not be technically correct to speak of this as a duty or obligation. *Karunā* is the free movement of *mushin*, and it does not require deontology. As Nishitani Keiji explained it, "The sun in the sky makes no choices about where to shine its rays and shows no preferences as to likes or dislikes. There is no selfishness in its shining. This lack of selfishness is what is meant by non-ego, or 'emptiness' (*śūnyāta*)."[30]

Karunā was a chief concern of the great Rinzai Zen reformer Hakuin. He had been an assiduous practitioner and achieved *satori* at a relatively early stage. This experience filled him with pride, and it was not until much later, after he achieved an even deeper *satori*, that he realized that *satori* is not some kind of personal achievement or a job well done. Deep *satori* is not something that happens to a person. In the eclipse of the ego's reign, it is the becoming Other-centered.

Hakuin was famous for being a severe critic of lazy, "do-nothing Zen". He had no patience for monks who just sat around and meditated. Meditation was for the sake of *kenshō*, enlightenment, but *kenshō* was not a personal accomplishment. It was the awakening of *karunā* from the ashes of the ego. Reflecting, as we have seen, that his original motivation for meditating had been to avoid hell, he laughed in appreciation when his disciple Tōrei later told him that his motivation for meditation was "To work for the salvation of my fellow beings." Hakuin admitted that this was "A much better reason than mine."[31] In his old age, Hakuin became a tireless teacher, working, as Fukushima indefatigably does, "To devote my energy to liberating the countless suffering beings of the world by imparting the great gift of the *dharma*; to

---

30. *Religion and Nothingness*, trans. Jan van Bragt (Berkeley: University of California Press, 1982), 60.
31. WI, xxii.

assemble a few select monks capable of passing through the barrier into genuine *kenshō*; to strive diligently toward creating conditions for the realization of a Buddha-land on earth and, in the process, carry into practice *Bodhisattva* vows."[32]

Fukushima explains that his calligraphy is "part of his compassion activity." This does not mean that it is something that he does in order to be compassionate. Rather it is the free movement of the great ocean of his Zen mind, no longer hindered by the aggressivity and narcissism of the ego. This is, I think, the most moving aspect of Fukushima's *zenki*. It is the gentle force, the kind of quiet storm, if you will, of Fukushima's style as it reaches out to alleviate the suffering of sentient beings.

---

32. WI, 84.

有花有月有楼台

素翁囑文又書堂人

Interview With Fukushima Rōshi

Fukushima Keidō Rōshi
Head Abbot of Tōfuku-ji Monastery

Jason M. Wirth
Interviewer

Jeff Shore
Professor of Zen Buddhism, Hanazono University, Kyoto, Interpreter

Interview: November 15 and 16, 2001, at Tōfuku-ji Monastery in Kyoto, Japan.

The first question is a very general question. Could you tell us something about the relationship between Zen and *shodō* (calligraphy)?

Zen priests usually cannot do calligraphy. However, almost all Zen Masters must do calligraphy. There are three basic ways that they write the Chinese characters. There is calligraphy accompanied by paintings. There is calligraphy written in Japanese. But the use of Chinese characters or *kanji* is the most common. To undergo Zen practice is to realize *mushin*, and the calligraphy of the Zen Master is an expression of that *mushin* activity, *mushin* in action.

Plate 18. Fukushima Keidō, *Ensō: There Are Flowers, There Is the Moon, There Is a Pavilion*, ink on paper, 13.5" x 53".

円相有花有月有樓台

Because Zen Masters have already completed their training, in general their calligraphy shows that well. There are some cases where the Zen Master's calligraphy is included in their Zen practice, but in terms of more formal calligraphic expressions, it can, in a sense, relax a little. For example, a professional calligrapher is often concerned with form—it is perhaps their greatest concern. However, when a Zen Master expresses himself through calligraphy, the main purpose is the expression of Zen mind, and hence the focus on form itself may relax somewhat. The main point of both Zen and Zen calligraphy is Zen mind. There is calligraphy done by professionals in which they take liberties with the form, but I think that it is better for the Zen Master to do this kind of thing. In so doing, he expresses his Zen mind, but he can also do it in a way that it can be appreciated by the professional calligrapher.

I think that it makes a difference if a Zen Master has had calligraphic training. Zen Master Hakuin [1686–1769] was a great calligrapher yet he did not have a lot of formal training. Some of his calligraphy is really free and really graceful. Yet since he did not undergo a lot of formal calligraphic training, one could misunderstand his calligraphy as sloppy. Actually Hakuin did spend a lot of time developing his own style, although he spent less doing so than would a professional calligrapher. Hakuin's Zen calligraphy is so great because not only has he developed his talent as a calligrapher, but also his Zen mind is perfectly expressed in his calligraphy. Hakuin's calligraphy is very unique, yet it is important to understand that he is not just arbitrarily breaking with form. One has to understand the relationship between form and the unique breaking of form. I think that it is unfortunate that sometimes the Zen priests and the Zen Masters, without sufficient technical training, simply try to imitate Hakuin's free, broken style. The same can be said about Zen Master Sengai. Both Sengai and Hakuin transcended formal calligraphic training. They are in some kind of Zen state of mind and really giving it full expression. When approaching Zen calligraphy, the emphasis has to be on the extent to which Zen mind is expressed in it.

A Zen Master who has already completed his Zen training and who has then developed technical calligraphic ability has the possibility of *shadatsu*,[1] which refers to going beyond the

---

1. *Shadatsu* is a classical term in Zen aesthetics that refers to the "unrestricted freedom" or the "lack of constraint" when one transcends rule and principle.

principle, transcending the rule. A Zen Master who is doing calligraphy is naturally express-ing his Zen mind and in so doing is transcending form.

Zen calligraphy really has to be the kind of calligraphy where you can get a feeling that you can see in it such a state of transcendence. It is important that the Zen expression comes from actual Zen experience. During my calligraphy demonstrations in the United States, I explain to students that this work is an expression of my own Zen mind. But then when the piece is shown to the students, sometimes one of them asks, "But where is the Zen mind?" I try to explain that it is in the totality, in the whole of the work, not in a single stroke or in an isolated part. In fact, it is to be found in the action of writing the Zen calligraphy—in the act itself. Professional calligraphers often prefer Zen calligraphy and like it very much. They find in it a charm or appeal because in it there is also a transcending of form. Once the form has been mastered, it is then "thrown away" or transcended. It is not thrown away from the begin-ning. It is hard to transcend form if one has not already undergone some formal training.

Many calligraphers in the history of calligraphy have said that calligraphy is not about the result but the process, and they often speak of *ki* or energy.[2] What do you think of the role of *ki* in your calligraphy?

Yes, *ki* is important in Zen calligraphy. *Ki* is not only found in the doing of the calligra-phy, but in the preparation of the ink and the spreading out of the paper. *Ki* has to be an expression of the total human being, not just something that comes out during a selected act. It is not something that you have to think about, nor is it something difficult to attain. It is naturally there in the Zen Master, not self-consciously. It is based on Zen experiences and practices, so I don't think that you will see that same kind of *ki* in a professional calligrapher.

Perhaps the key point to *ki* is concentration. Professional calligraphers self-con-sciously try to cultivate this *ki*, but in the Zen Master it is just something that is there nat-urally and that naturally finds expression. One difference between a Zen Master and a professional, technically competent calligrapher is that the Zen Master does one piece and *ki* is naturally there. The technical calligrapher keeps writing the character as he tries to develop *ki*.

---

2. *Ki* (Chinese: *ch'i*) is a central term in the Daoist and Buddhist traditions, denoting the universe's subtle energy or life force. Vide the essay immediately preceding this interview, "Bokki & Zen No Sho: Approaching the Work of Fukushima Keidō Rōshi."

Ki is also connected with breathing. Breathing when you are doing calligraphy is very important. Doing calligraphy is very free, but before I do a piece in such a state, I will just sit for a moment and compose myself. There is a certain kind of breathing that I first do, then I execute the piece. The focus is hence on breathing, and that *ki* goes out to the calligraphy through breathing.

Again, this is perhaps just my own style, but I do not do an *ensō* (Zen circle) quickly. I am rather doing it in accord with my breathing. So as I am going through my breathing and I am softly exhaling, I am completing the *ensō*. While perhaps this is just my own style, it is very important that when doing calligraphy I am doing it with my breathing, with my *ki*, and that they are overflowing and coming to expression.

I don't do martial arts myself, but in watching certain kinds, it seems that the practitioners take the *ki* and hold it and then, in performing a certain act, a certain form, they are, in a sense, loosening the *ki*. I understand that methodology. There is a similar connection between calligraphy and *ki*.

But again, the point is that this is not something that we are preoccupied with and self-conscious about. It happens naturally and then it comes out in the work. It is important that this happens naturally. If one tries to do this self-consciously when, for example, one self-consciously tries to do a really powerful piece, a manipulation and a thought process is still present, and hence the piece will not be a natural expression. Some calligraphers are able to do calligraphy like the natural flowing of water. That is how Zen Masters strive to do it.

Most of the great Zen calligraphers have had a very individual and particular style. How would you describe your individual and particular style? Where did it come from and what are its characteristics?

I trained under two different Zen Masters. When I met my first Zen Master, Okada Rōshi [of Hōfuku-ji] when I was fourteen years old, I had already learned the fundamentals of calligraphy. If you already have the basics of calligraphy under your belt, so to speak, then you can really learn a lot from being around and working with a Zen Master. A Zen monk training at a monastery does not have the time to practice and develop his own style. But I worked

Plate 19. Fukushima Keidō, *Ensō: No Guest or Host*, ink on paper, 13.5" x 53".

円相無賓主

with and assisted Okada Rōshi for ten years, and during that time I was able to learn how to imitate his style. Okada Rōshi used the *kaisho* ("block" or "regular") style, although I now use the *gyōsho* ("semi-cursive" or "running") style.[3]

I later studied under my second Master, Shibayama Rōshi, and learned from his calligraphy style, and I then came to do my calligraphy in his style, which led to my present use of the *gyōsho* style. I really came to like this *gyōsho* style. With *gyōsho*, as well as with *sōsho*, rhythm is more important than with *kaisho*. Shibayama really taught me this. Watching Shibayama do calligraphy, I could see his whole body and mind concentrating. I do not know if he was conscious of it or not, but looking at him, one could see his rhythm. So just as when a train starts, it begins slowly, then gradually builds up speed, I also unconsciously begin slowly and build up speed. It was the same way with Shibayama Rōshi. He would get into a rhythm after awhile and start humming to himself. I also unconsciously start humming. When I do my calligraphy here in my room in the monastery, I begin humming and I do not realize that I might be disturbing people. Only the senior monks can come down the hallway by my room, and sometimes they will tell me that they can hear me humming while I am doing my calligraphy. They told me that they noticed that what I am now humming is different from what I used to hum. In the old days I used to sing a song about Lake Biwa.[4] Now they hear me humming the [American] national anthem, just as Shibayama Rōshi did.

---

3. Japanese calligraphy (*shodō*) generally follows Chinese traditional calligraphy (*shu*) and tends to rely on *kanji* (a Japanese term which literally means "Chinese characters"). *Kaisho* (Chinese: *kai shu* or *zheng shu*) is the so-called "block" script. It is the standard or regular script and is typically used to teach calligraphy because it demands correct character formation and brush use. Ancient scripts include *tensho* or "seal" script, the oldest of scripts, and *reisho*, or "clerical" script. The most abstract and difficult-to-read style is *sōsho* or "cursive" script (Chinese: *cao shu*), which originates in a radical abbreviation of Chinese characters. *Sōsho* is called the "grass" style and it has the appearance of a kind of quickly executed rough sketch of a character done with an ink-saturated brush in a single stroke. Fukushima Rōshi employs *gyōsho* (Chinese: *xing shu*) or the "semi-cursive" style. Also called the "running" style, *gyōsho* does not simplify the character to the same extent, although it, too, is executed in a single stroke with a heavily inked brush. Its origins lie with perhaps the greatest of all Chinese calligraphers, Wang Xizhi of the fourth century C.E., whose masterpiece, *Orchid Pavilion Preface* (*Lan Ting Xu*), among other magnificent works, set the standard for the running style. The *gyōsho* style was a semi-cursive development of the block or *kaisho* style, and in it strokes merge one into the other. The grass style emerged from the *gyōsho* style and it speeds across the paper, greatly simplifying the characters. Zen calligraphy traditionally employs either *kaisho* or *gyōsho* or *sōsho*, with *kaisho* being the least popular and *sōsho* being the most popular. Hisamatsu reminds us, however, that even when Zen Masters use the seemingly conservative *kaisho*, they do not use it in a traditional or conservative way: "the overall feeling is never one of regularity, but rather of distortion" (Hisamatsu, *Zen and the Fine Arts*, 67). For further discussion of these styles, vide Dr. Addiss's essay.

4. The largest freshwater lake in Japan, Biwa is found in the vicinity of Kyoto.

Calligraphy has often been compared to dance as its closest and most similar art form. Do you find this to be a good or helpful comparison?

I can see some comparison when one thinks of calligraphy's rhythmic elements, although I still think that calligraphy is much closer to painting. There may be some connections to dance, but I do not think that I would put them too closely together. I can understand, however, why some people would speak of calligraphy in that way. If one were to compare it to dance, it would certainly not be a fast dance. It would be more of a slow dance. Comparing it to something like Michael Jackson's moonwalk [*laughter*], even if such a dance were done slowly, I would have to say that Zen calligraphy is much different.

Yet you can detect some similarities between Zen calligraphy and dance. Since I do not dance myself, I perhaps cannot see all of these similarities. If I did dance I would perhaps see a lot more connections. There are, however, some exceptions. During certain times in *dokusan* (*kōan* training),[5] I may do some dancing. [*Laughter*]. There is a moment in *dokusan* in which doing calligraphy in *mushin* would be a good answer. But if a monk simply imitates doing calligraphy in *mushin* rather than actually doing calligraphy in *mushin*, then that answer would be automatically rejected.

Why do you prefer *gyōsho* rather than *sōsho* or *kaisho*? What do you personally like about *gyōsho*?

When I studied with my first Master, Okada Rōshi, *kaisho* was all that I knew and I liked it very much. But when I studied with my second Master, Shibayama Rōshi, I learned *gyōsho*, and when I compared *kaisho* with *gyōsho*, I found that I preferred the *gyōsho* style. When I do calligraphy, it is something very pleasant and enjoyable. What appealed to me about the *kaisho* of my first Master was that it was written in a very slow style. Also there is a certain way of writing *kaisho* where you hold in the *ki* until you get to a place where you can turn it and loosen the *ki* at that point.[6] I could follow and appreciate that. I think that the characteristic of my first Master was to be in a very quiet mind and then to do this *kaisho* very slowly, so that

---

5. *Dokusan* is an integral part of Zen training, especially for the Rinzai sect, of which Fukushima is a member. It literally means "to go alone to a high one" and in practice it is a private ("to go alone") meeting between a Rōshi ("a high one") and an acolyte for *kōan* training.

6. Classically, *kaisho* is executed in the rhythm called *ton-sū-ton*, stop-move-stop. One writes in rhythmic alterations of hold-release-hold-release…

is what I first came to like. What I came to like about my second Master and his *gyōsho* was that there was something very dynamic about it. I think the basis for his *gyōsho* was the dynamism already found in Zen, and this calligraphic style exhibits that characteristic.

One of the characteristics of classical Western art is symmetry and balance. One of the characteristics of Asian art tends to be the opposite: dynamic asymmetry. How important is dynamic asymmetry to your calligraphy?[7]

There are many kinds of calligraphy, and some of them are very symmetrical while some of them are not. I prefer and tend more towards the symmetrical. Take for example the calligraphy of my second Master, Shibayama Rōshi. [*Fukushima points to a framed work of calligraphy by Shibayama.*] It is very rhythmic and dynamic, yet it is also very symmetrical. I also have here a work of calligraphy by a contemporary Chan Master who died last year. It, too, is very symmetrical.

There of course were many great Zen Masters whose calligraphy was irregular and asymmetrical, but rather than calling these works asymmetrical, I think that it is better to say that they transcend symmetry and asymmetry. I think among the many great Chinese calligraphy Masters, there were some who were able to transcend symmetry, but that is only after many years of calligraphy practice. Perhaps there is even some kind of conscious desire to want eventually to transcend symmetry. For myself, at least at this point in my life, I do not want to transcend symmetry. I am rather fond of it.

I think that the desire to transcend or not to transcend symmetry is connected to the particular Zen Master's lifestyle. There are some Zen Masters who have an almost violent lifestyle that is in itself a kind of breaking with symmetry. I think that in the T'ang Dynasty (618–907 C.E.) there were several Chan monks who had that kind of violent lifestyle and consequently violent calligraphy. They had very decent calligraphy, and it came to be favored and people

---

7. This is for example the contention of Sōetsu Yanagi, who in *The Unknown Craftsman: A Japanese Insight into Beauty*, argued that "freedom always resolves into irregularity in the end. 'Free' beauty of necessity boils down to irregular beauty" (Tokyo: Kodansha International, revised edition, 1989), 119. Irregularity is most associated with the "grass" or "cursive" style, although it is important to note that the conscious cultivation of either regularity or irregularity does not belong to the free play of Zen calligraphy.

Plate 20. Fukushima Keidō, *Ensō: Watch, Touch and Bite*, ink on paper, 13.5" x 53".

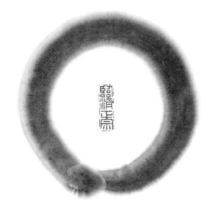

Watch
touch
and
bite

Japan
Keido

wanted to imitate it. That is not a bad thing. But I think that both my first and second Master consciously disliked "unnatural" and violent things. If there was a Zen monk with this kind of "unnatural" attitude, which is not at all a bad thing, both of my Masters tended to dislike him, so I myself also developed an aversion to consciously "unnatural" things. This lifestyle, which, for want of a better word, I am calling "unnatural," influences their calligraphy.

Again, when I use these words "natural" and "unnatural," I am not saying that one is good and the other is bad.[8] In the end it is up to the observer to decide which style he prefers. For example, if you take the *ensō*, you can see that some people consciously try to avoid making one that is symmetrically round, preferring rather something that is irregular. Both of my Masters made a relatively round *ensō*. When a real Master makes an irregular *ensō*, it is not like he is trying to purposively mess it up. That is just his style. Hakuin's calligraphy in his later years had this kind of irregular and unnatural style. He is an example of someone who had really mastered the form and who was hence able to break the form. But if there is a priest who is simply trying to imitate externally that unnaturalness, that breaking of the form just hurts your eyes. Hakuin is different. When he breaks the form, it really engages you. In Hakuin's case he was *naturally* doing it unnaturally, but in the Zen priest's case he is just *unnaturally* doing something unnatural. He is just arbitrarily trying to do something unnatural.

In the Zen tradition, language is a big problem, and many Zen Masters are duly suspicious of language. The notorious difficulty of *dharma* transmission reminds us how seriously this tradition takes the problem of communication. How important is it to Zen calligraphy to read what is written? To what extent is an appreciation of Zen calligraphy tied to what is literally written in the work?

Most Zen calligraphy uses only Chinese characters (*kanji*). Zen calligraphers use traditional Zen expressions, and this is because the calligraphy has a pedagogical element. So it is

---

8. The "natural" is a term used in English to try and capture some of the nuances of the critical Zen aesthetic term *sabi*, the unforced and graceful and free expression of Zen mind. It cannot be consciously cultivated but is rather the free movement of the Zen mind's creativity.

Plate 21. Attributed to Sesshū Tōyō (1420–1506), *Bodhidharma*, ink on paper, 33" x 75.75."

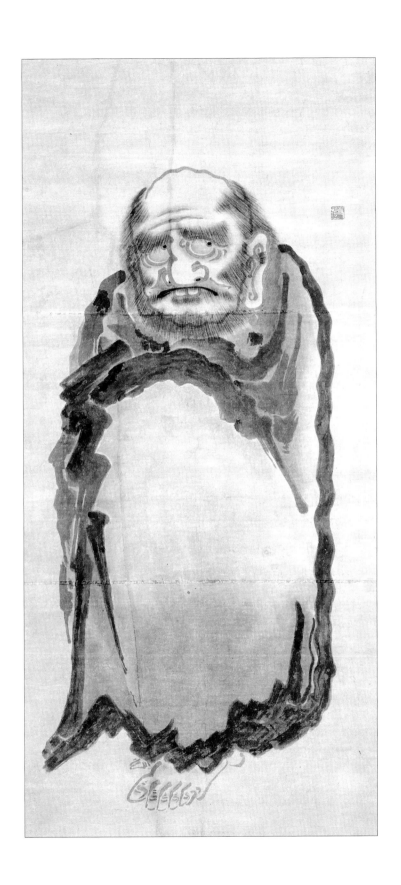

not just an attractive artwork, there is something behind it. For example, *Nichi nichi kore ko nichi* ("Every day is a fine day") is a traditional Zen teaching that goes back to Ummon.

But if someone were just to look at a work of Zen calligraphy and not have any idea what it says, is that a bad thing?

Certainly if you can't read the calligraphy at all, you can grasp the dynamism of the Zen Master's Zen mind. However, if you can understand the characters and their Zen meaning, that is even better.

The famous T'ang Dynasty calligrapher Sun Qianli claimed in his *Shu Pu* (*Treatise on Calligraphy*, 687 C.E.), "Ordinary people could not recognize the musical potential in the sound of a burning piece of wood."[9] When they hear wood burning, they don't hear music. They just hear wood burning. Sun thought that one needed a special ear, a kind of Zen ear, if you will, to hear what the ordinary mind cannot hear. You said tonight, of course, to do calligraphy, you need Zen mind. By analogy with Sun, do you need Zen mind to appreciate or "see" calligraphy?

It is certainly better if the person appreciating the work of calligraphy has Zen mind. And it would be best if the person appreciating it also had the same mind as the one doing the work. I think that another way of explaining why I came to like and appreciate the calligraphy of Shibayama Rōshi so much is that I came to have the same mind that he had. For example, in the Zen tradition they speak of *dharma* transmission, and there is an expression that brings out what I am trying to say: "Unless the mind of the disciple is in some way the same as the mind of the Master, the transmission cannot take place." This is very much connected to art as well.

It is better, of course, that someone does have some Zen mind, and the closer it is to my mind, the more they will be able to appreciate my work. For example, consider Jōshū, the great T'ang Dynasty Chan Master. His writings and *teishō*,[10] collected in the *Jōshū Record*,[11] really show the fullness of the Zen mind that he developed over many years. I feel that in

---

9. In *Two Chinese Treatises on Calligraphy*, trans. Chang Ch'ung-ho and Hans H. Frankel (New Haven: Yale University Press, 1995), 15.

10. *Teishō*, meaning "presentation" or "offering," usually takes place during intensive meditation (*sesshin*) and is a presentation of the Zen Master's *mushin*. Often, although it need not, it deals with a *kōan* in which commentary is offered that presents the depth of the Master's realized mind.

11. Vide *The Recorded Sayings of Zen Master Jōshū*, trans. James Green (Boston: Shambhala, 1998). Fukushima Rōshi has intimated that he plans to publish an extensive *teishō* on the *Jōshū Record*. Jōshū (Chinese: Chao-chou Ts'ung-shen, 778–897) originated the famous *mu kōan* ("Does a dog have Buddha-nature?") that is often the initial *kōan* for *dokusan*.

order for me to approach the mind of Jōshū, I need another ten or twenty years. If Jōshū were here now and he saw my calligraphy, he would probably say that it is not that good. If someone who had a little bit of Zen mind were to see my calligraphy, they might think that it was pretty good. If they had the same level of Zen mind, they might find that it was perfect, complete. But if they had Jōshū 's level of Zen mind, which has gone far beyond my own Zen mind, they would probably think that it wasn't so hot. [*Laughter*]

Who in your opinion is the greatest Zen calligrapher?

Hakuin.

Your Master, Shibayama, claimed in his *Flower Does Not Talk*, "True art should be the spiritual motivation to awaken deep humanity at the bottom of reality."[12] What do you think he meant by this, and how does your calligraphy try to awaken deep humanity?

I think in Zen as a religion as well as in Zen art, the spirituality of the Zen Master must be expressed and it must come out in the work. So this deep spirituality, which comes out of both the Master's humanity and individuality, is not something that can be imitated or followed. It is not the result of following certain rules or styles.

That is why each individual's unique expression of this spirituality will come into form in both his artistic and religious work. For example there are Zen Masters who will pound on the table—whack!—and exclaim, "This is Zen!" Of course this a valid and authentic expression of Zen, but both of my Zen Masters did not prefer this kind of expression. They were more interested in making Zen teaching available and comprehensible to the general public. If you do this more extreme kind of act, only a few people can grasp it or fathom it. My teachers went to great lengths to try and interpret Zen activity so that a greater audience could appreciate them. This naturally comes to expression in the way that folks express their religion as well as their art. For example, in a Zen art expression, the total person comes into form, and that has very much to do with Zen training and practice. If that does not happen, it is not going to be Zen art. In all elements of Zen life, including Zen artistic expression, the full embodiment comes out. Another way of putting it is that it is a question of being something fully. It is a question of *samādhi*[13] or concentration, and *mushin*, to be totally whatever it is that one is

---

12. Shibayama, *A Flower Does Not Talk*, trans. Sumiko Kudo (Kyoto: Nanzen-ji, 1967), 52–53. This essay is now in print with Charles Tuttle.

13. *Samādhi* is the original Sanskrit term for the settling of the mind so that there is total concentration on a single object. In so doing, the bifurcation between the subject who meditates and the object of meditation is overcome.

doing at the time, so that the work comes from this. Zen art must come to expression in the same way. Take for example Chan Master Jōshū and his *mu*. That was a perfect expression of his full embodiment of *mu* at the time.

More to the point, Zen mind will express itself in an individual in a unique way, but it is important that Zen art originates in this Zen mind. Or to put it another way, the Zen power comes out in the total person, not just in a particular aspect of their art. The Zen power of the total person comes to a unique expression in a particular art. I cannot think of a better example of this than Hakuin. So many people have commented that Hakuin's calligraphy is so unique to him. It is so powerful that sometimes you may see a certain piece, and it almost turns you off. It's so overflowing with this kind of uniqueness. Again that has to do with his total embodiment. It is said that another Zen Master like Hakuin will not appear for 500 years.

You once said that one of the best compliments to your calligraphy was that your stroke was similar to that of the great Sesshū Tōyō (1420–1506). Could you describe your relationship to Sesshū? What made Sesshū great? What do you like about him? How is he similar to you?

I was very fortunate that the first place that I trained as an acolyte monk was in a temple [Hōfuku-ji in Okayama] where Sesshū himself had lived and worked. In my case, when I was fourteen and I first went there, I was able to see with my own eyes some of the National Treasures that Sesshū had painted.[14] There are ten works by Sesshū still at this temple and five of them are National Treasures. The National Treasures are not that big. When I first saw one of the simpler National Treasure paintings, I was fourteen years old and I knew nothing about Zen but I thought that I would like to do something like that. I just looked at it and thought, "Oh yeah, there is a mountain and a river and a boat." I thought the fine, delicate detail was more difficult in this kind of painting. Everything uses simple strokes. Only after studying Buddhism and then doing Buddhist practice was I able to appreciate the depth found in Sesshū. So when I was fourteen or fifteen years old and still in junior high school, I came to

---

14. The designation National Treasure officially protects works of paramount cultural value.

Plate 22. Shibayama Zenkei and D. T. Suzuki (1869–1966), *Wondrous* [right side, done by Suzuki] and *Making Fire in Water* [left side, done by Shibayama], ink on paper, 19.5" x 11.25".

妙　火向水中焚

妙

大拙

中华
生白
牛

丙戌
金芳

大拙

like painting more than calligraphy. When the Master was not around, I would often go and look at the Sesshū paintings. The reason that only five of the ten paintings are designated National Treasures is because they have been authenticated. The other five are just reputed to be by Sesshū.

One of the five that is only reputed to be by Sesshū is a big and powerful portrait of Bodhidharma (Daruma) (**Plate 21, page 89**).[15] Even though it's not a National Treasure, it is the Sesshū painting that I like the best. One of the things I like about it is that it is very rare for a Bodhidharma to be depicted as standing in such a manner that you can see his feet, and in this painting you can see Bodhidharma's two feet sticking out. Even the toenails are depicted in detail. I was really overwhelmed the first time I saw it. I think when you see it you will understand what I first saw in it myself. I was so overwhelmed with the power of the way that the feet were painted. They had such power and they drew me in all the way up to the toenail. Such a distinctive power!

I think this painting affected my calligraphy. Such a pointed power with those feet—I can't explain it—but when I sign my works now, at the end I paint a long line that actually comes from the impact that the painting of Bodhidharma's toenail had on me. When I saw the painting again while I was in graduate school at Ōtani University, it already had lost the initial impact that it had on me when I first saw it. Yet I still think the painting as a whole remains very powerful. I think that it was really great in my cultivation as an artist to be in the presence of these Sesshū paintings. When I was in junior high school, we made greeting cards and on mine I did an imitation of Sesshū. Although they did not recognize the particular painting that I was imitating, they knew that I was an acolyte monk in the monastery where Sesshū had lived. Even though I no longer do any painting, he has influenced my calligraphy.

There is a similarity between painting and calligraphy. Empty space is important for both. In calligraphy the space around the characters is very important, and that is also true for Sesshū. I think that a person who looks at both can pick up on the similarities. I think that one of the reasons that American audiences tend to like the *ensō* is not because of the circular shape but because of the empty space inside of it. I suspect that if you filled in the *ensō*, people would not like it.

---

15. Bodhidharma was the twenty-eighth patriarch and in the fifth century C.E. is credited with bringing the *dharma* to China and hence becoming the first Chinese patriarch. Fukushima is referring to the Sesshū portrait of Bodhidharma in this show (**Plate 21, page 88**).

I have a two-part question: You once claimed that becoming a monk "was not just for the sake of family, but for the whole world."[16] I would first like to ask you what you meant, and then I would like to ask you how such compassion relates to art.

I myself had a personal reason why I became a monk. It goes back to my childhood, when my older sister passed away and then my grandmother, who was like a mother to me, passed away shortly thereafter. While I was studying classical Chinese literature in school, I learned that if someone becomes a monk, they can save nine generations of their family and send them to the Pure Land. This belief was not actually in any textbook, but the teacher had written it on the chalkboard. Afterwards I came to see that one does not become a monk for personal reasons but for the sake of all sentient beings. One of the reasons that a Zen Master does calligraphy is for the sake of ordinary people. Calligraphy is one way of presenting Zen teaching, and that in a sense is one of my "compassion activities." But I do not think that there is any privileged relationship between calligraphy and compassion.

Can you tell us more about the significance of the *ensō*, both traditionally and for you personally?

The *ensō* is a classic symbol of Zen. You could say that it is a kind of symbolic expression of *satori*. A circle—not the depicted *ensō*, but a circle as such—has a kind of perfect roundness and yet is empty on the inside. There is a famous painting by Sengai that depicts a circle, a square, and a triangle, but it was the circle that was the most accomplished expression of Zen mind. This goes all the way back to the T'ang Dynasty in which the Chan monks, instead of using Chinese characters, would use a circle. Indeed there was something about a circle, more so than either a square or a triangle, that expressed more fully the state of *satori*. Even when you are writing Zen phrases using *kanji*, you are in a state of *mushin* empty mind. There is just something about the *ensō* that more naturally captures the fullness of this state of mind. Sometimes one draws a long line, as in a stick,[17] but still the *ensō* always seems a fuller expression.

---

16. Quoted in Seo and Addiss, *The Art of Twentieth-Century Zen*, 178.

17. Fukushima is referring to the *mujibō*, the Zen line, or the line that expresses *mu*. As Ōmori Sōgen and Terayama Katsujō explain, "A *mujibō* is like a decisive cut of a live sword in a fight to the finish; it slices the universe in two. As the samurai classic *Hagakure* states: 'Shatter the paper with your brush when you write!' If anything is held back there can be no *mujibō*. One Master of the past refused to accept anyone who was not drenched in sweat after writing one *mujibō*." *Zen and the Art of Calligraphy: The Essence of Sho*, trans. John Stevens (New York and London: Viking Penguin, 1990), 94.

And how about your personal relationship to the *ensō*? You often paint them.

Yes, that is my favorite expression of Zen mind. Some people might think that merely drawing circles is Zen art, but it is important to remember that the *ensō* is always accompanied by a Zen saying or expression and that one has to take the work as a whole into account.

If one were to go to, say, Nikkō and see the famous Tokugawa mausoleums,[18] one could never say that they were the products of Zen mind. They are very busy and crowded and ornate. Zen art has always had the opposite tendency. Why does Zen art strive to say more with less?

Zen art is based on *śūnyāta* or emptiness,[19] and hence it always tends towards simplicity and is indeed the opposite of a place like Nikkō. The latter is more like the intellectual quality of some Western art, which tends to bring out the ego.

Would it ever be possible for there to be a complicated or ornate work of Zen art?

This is certainly possible. Just because it is Zen art, this does not mean that it *has* to be simple. *Śūnyāta* does not mean that the world is empty of things. It is an emptiness that contains everything, so it is entirely possible that it could be expressed in a complex form. Still, the basis would be the same as in all Zen art, namely *mushin* empty mind.

Can one define Zen art as art done in a true Zen mind? If that is so, can anything, if it is done in Zen mind, be Zen art? Or, is it restricted to the traditional art forms like *sumi-e* (ink painting), *shodō*, *kadō* (*ikebana*, flower arranging), *chadō* (tea ceremony), etc.?

I guess the question is whether any act could be considered Zen art or not. For example, if you take sumo wrestling, there is a kind of *mushin* present there, but I still would not call that art. It really is more of a sport. However, in something like Nō drama, when someone in *mushin* plays the flute, this playing is a form of Zen art. On the other hand, there might be somebody who, without Zen training, unconsciously does something with *mushin*. Although

---

18. Located not far from Tokyo, Nikkō is the site of the grand mausoleums and shrines that were built in the seventeenth century to bury and honor the patriarchs of the Tokugawa clan. Fifteen thousand artisans were used to construct the structures, and they are highly ornate—a kind of Japanese rococo honor to the great political power and immense wealth of the Tokugawa clan.

19. The Mahāyāna traditions holds that all things are "empty" or "void" of intrinsic nature or essence. They do not have their own being, *svabhāva*, and hence are free of substantial natures. Hence the Sanskrit term *śūnyāta* or emptiness.

Plate 23. Okada Rōshi, *Don't Have Wrong Thought*, ink on paper, 16" x 14".

幕妄想

they might not even be aware when they are dancing or painting that they are in *mushin*, a trained monk might be able to see that they are.

Is it possible, when in Zen mind, to come up with new forms of art?

Although Zen can certainly produce new forms of art, I think that it has already come into quite full fruition in the traditional art forms and I think that we should continue with them. In something like [Michael Jackson's] moonwalk or in some forms of progressive dancing, for example, there may be an element of *mushin*, but that does not therefore make it Zen art. There must be categories of traditional art and there must be the coming to expression of Zen mind within those traditions.

Does one need to be a Zen Master or even a Zen practitioner to paint good or even great Zen art? Can one have the right Zen mind without long training? How does one explain that artists who were not monks or priests or Zen Masters did some important Zen art?

As you say, one does not have to be a Zen Master or monk to do Zen art. Even a layperson who has some training can develop *mushin* and in this state produce art. But in principle, the deeper and the longer the training, the better. Take for example Sesshū, who was an extremely talented and marvelous artist. But he was also a Zen monk who had even trained in China. It is really important to have Zen training and Zen experience. I think that if you had two people, a layperson without Zen training and a monk in Zen training, and they were both to draw an *ensō*, a Zen Master would be able to see that one *ensō* expressed some Zen mind and the other did not. The person without the Zen training would be intent on trying to make a perfect *ensō* and in a sense be attached to that, and the Zen Master would be able to see that. The monk would be beyond that.

When one looks at the history of the great Rōshis in the Chinese and Japanese and Korean traditions, one notices many unique features, but one of the common features tends to be extensive playfulness and a good sense of humor. That certainly is true of you. What is the relationship between playfulness or humor and Zen in general as well as in your calligraphy in particular?

I once gave a lecture on Zen and humor. With such a lecture, there are plenty of opportunities to recount all kinds of funny stories. But there is also a philosophical dimension. Much of what a Zen Master does has an element of humor and playfulness to it because they have transcended dualistic thinking. Having done so, they are not so attached to the fruits of dualistic thinking, such as, for example, this is good and that is bad. They are free of such attachments because they know that no good is absolutely and in all ways good. For example, everyone may want a certain kind of teacup and become very attached to acquiring one. But the Zen Master, precisely because he is not attached to anything, can say, "Fine, I do not want one. You can have it!" Having transcended dualistic thinking endows the Zen Master with a certain playfulness. If a person has undergone Zen training, a sense of humor may come out in their Zen personality. Take for example my two Masters, Shibayama Rōshi and Okada Rōshi. Shibayama did not joke around a lot. Of course he had a sense of humor, but he did not really express it often. Okada Rōshi, on the other hand, was a very humorous person.

Is there any playfulness and humor in your calligraphy?

No, I do not have any conscious intention of doing my calligraphy in that frame of mind, but there is nonetheless an element of humor inherent in many of the Zen expressions that I use. An exception is when I do calligraphy in the States, and I do it in English and paint an *ensō* and intentionally use a humorous phrase like, "Please eat this."

Can you speak about the *dō* (or *dao*) in *shodō*?

Shodō means the way of calligraphy, while a word like *chadō* means the way of tea, and *kadō* means the way of flowers. The *dō* is the Chinese *dao*, but this does not speak to a specific technique for doing these things. It speaks to the spiritual depths from which these art forms arise. It is necessary to understand the depth of this "path" or "way." This "way" is critical to both Zen and Zen arts.

Can you speak to the danger of the ego to art? Is the ego a barrier to good art of any kind, not just Zen art, and would this not indict a lot of Western art?

Of course the ego is a big problem for any art. I think that one of the tendencies in some Western art is to be rather intellectual, and if one is intellectual, the ego tends to come out in one's work more. Good art comes from a pure mind. If someone wants to self-consciously do a painting just because they want to see it one day exhibited in the Tokyo National Museum, they are painting with a defiled mind. One should not focus on oneself so much when one is doing art.

Zen traditionally teaches freedom from attachment. What do you make of the fact that, for example, if one has a piece of calligraphy or a painting by Ikkyū or Sesshū or Hakuin or Sengai, then everybody wants to have it. Such things become very valuable. So when they paint they are free from attachment, but they produce a work that everybody is attached to. What do you make of this?

Of course, what you say is true, but the problem is not on the side of Sesshū or Ikkyū or Hakuin. It really is a paradox. A really great and true artist is not doing their work in order to be admired, but that is precisely what is so appealing to the audience. They can sense that in the painting, and hence they come to desire it and get wrapped up in their own attachments.

What do you hope Westerners will learn from your calligraphy?

If they can move through the calligraphy and get to the point in which they can see the Zen mind underlying it, I think that would be good.

What advice do you have for Americans who are interested in Buddhist practice?

On the one hand, the United States is making a very important advance on traditional Buddhism in the case of women. For the first time, women and men are represented in Buddhism in equal numbers and, compared to other Buddhist traditions, women are treated in American Buddhism in a kind of ideal and democratic way. I think that this is an important advance for Buddhism.

On the other hand, new things easily seduce Americans, just because they are new. They sometimes think that just because something is new, it must be better. And since American Zen comes largely from Japan, Japanese Zen is a kind of older brother to American Zen and has to keep a watchful eye on it. When something new comes along that is clearly not something better, like *dokusan* by telephone or the Internet, it is important for us to help our younger brother.

Do you think that the American lay tradition can flourish without the monastic tradition?

If you have a chance as a layperson to study at a monastery as a kind of shortcut to Zen experience, that is a good thing, but I do not think that a layperson has to study at a monastery in order to have Zen experience. I think that it is up to the individual to choose. I think that there is some danger in the United States of incomplete Zen Masters, so one has to be careful with whom one studies. I hope that Americans will get past the problem of incomplete Zen Masters.

I want to thank you for all that you do for us.

Thank you very much!

Plate 24. Shibayama Rōshi, *Nothing Is Everything, Everything Is Nothing*, ink on paper, 12.75" x 52".

空即是色 色即是空

The Main Gate (a National Treasure) of Tōfuku-ji Monastery.

Tōfuku-ji Monastery
A BRIEF HISTORICAL SKETCH

Ronald L. Carlisle

The Tōfuku-ji Monastery in Kyoto is one of the largest and historically most significant of all Japanese Zen Buddhist monasteries. Since its founding nearly 800 years ago, Tōfuku-ji has been the home and training ground of thousands of Zen monks and priests. It has been a vital force in shaping the cultural life of Japan. The monastery has enjoyed numerous close ties with Japan's artistic, military, political, and merchant leaders. Today, although Tōfuku-ji is especially popular among tourists, it remains a training monastery for Zen priests and is the site of hundreds of artistic masterpieces, including many that are recognized as National Treasures by the Japanese government.

Tōfuku-ji was originally conceived and built in 1235 by the regent Kujō Michiie (1193–1252). The new Buddhist monastery in Kyoto was to rival the great Nara monasteries of Tōdai-ji and Kōfuku-ji, a fact that is reflected in its very name. That Michiie was a high-ranking courtier is emblematic of the exceptionally close relationship that existed between Tōfuku-ji and the emperor's court, the titular rulers of Japan, alongside its connections with the shogunate, the actual wielders of power.

The Zen sect of Buddhism had been introduced to Japan from China by the monk Myōan Eisai (1141–1215) barely fifty years before the founding of Tōfuku-ji, and at the time was a far distant second in importance to the established Shingon and Tendai sects. Indeed, Michiie almost surely did not conceive of Tōfuku-ji as a Zen monastery, but rather as a great temple to the Buddhist establishment of his time. Michiie chose Enni Ben'en (1202–1280) to be Tōfuku-ji's first Abbot. Although Enni was firmly grounded in Tendai Buddhism, he was also very sympathetic toward Zen, with which he had become familiar during his studies in Song Dynasty China. Accordingly, at the beginning, Tōfuku-ji embodied a syncretic blend of Shingon and Tendai with Zen Buddhism, from the character of its religious observances to its architectural features. Persons of a wide range of Buddhist persuasions would have felt comfortable and uplifted in the surroundings afforded by Enni's Tōfuku-ji. This was another important factor in the monastery's early success and rapid growth.

Zen, although a relative newcomer to Japan, rapidly gained in popularity, especially among the ruling military class. The austere, self-reliant, non-intellectual nature of Zen appealed to the medieval warrior. As a result, many Zen monasteries were established in Kamakura, the seat of the thirteenth- and early-fourteenth-century shogunate, as well as in Kyoto, the imperial capital. Tōfuku-ji followed that trend, soon becoming almost exclusively a Zen institution. This process was aided by fire, the perennial scourge of Japanese buildings, which historically were constructed almost exclusively of wood. Fire destroyed all of the original thirteenth-century buildings, and their replacements were firmly in the Zen mold.

Zen was inherited from China, and the Japanese constantly sought to model their Zen on the Chinese original, especially as it flourished during the Sung Dynasty. Japanese monks traveled to China and returned to Japan with the knowledge of Sung Zen with which to shape monastic practices as well as the physical characteristics of the newly emerging monasteries. Equally important, many Chinese Masters were brought to Japan to serve as abbots and otherwise direct the development of the Zen foundations in Japan.

The crucial notion of the *gozan*, or five mountains, was adopted very early in the history of Japanese Zen. Borrowing from Sung China, Zen monasteries were commonly referred to as mountains. Sometimes the monasteries were actually situated on mountains, but more commonly the mountain designation symbolized their being apart from the ordinary secular world. Continuing to borrow from China, the shogunate began to recognize the most influential of the Rinzai Zen monasteries as being members of the *gozan*; Rinzai was one of the two major Buddhist sects in Japan, the other being Sōtō. Typically there were somewhat more than five monasteries recognized as *gozan*, with monasteries in both Kamakura and Kyoto being granted

Zendo Hall and Kyozo Hall, Tōfuku-ji Monastery.

that status. Membership in the *gozan* shifted quite frequently, but Tōfuku-ji was always included in that ranking. Tōfuku-ji was unusual among the *gozan* monasteries in that the abbots were always to be chosen from among the spiritual descendents of Enni, the founding Abbot. Abbots for most of the other *gozan* monasteries were chosen, by the shogunate, from qualified candidates of any Zen lineage. Tōfuku-ji was able to maintain this bit of independence from the military rulers in large part thanks to its early and uniquely strong ties with the court.

The layout of the great Zen monasteries and the architecture of their buildings were heavily influenced by models established in Sung China. Tōfuku-ji is no exception, and in fact is one of the clearest examples of Sung Zen's impact on the physical appearance of Japanese monasteries. Accordingly, Tōfuku-ji was, and remains, oriented around a north-south axis. The main gate, or mountain gate as it is appropriately called, lies on the south end of the axis. This very impressive structure grandly marks the entrance to the monastery and symbolizes the passage from the outside world to the cloistered realm. Just north of the mountain gate, to the west of the axis lies first the latrine and next the monks' hall. The monks' hall traditionally

The Southern Garden of the Abbot's Hall, Tōfuku-ji Monastery.

was the communal residence of all the monks currently enrolled in the monastery. Each monk was allotted one tatami mat, a woven grass mat approximately three by six feet in size, as his living space. Each monk ate his meals, practiced *zazen* (seated meditation), took his tea, and slept on his mat. To the east of the central axis is the bathhouse, and to its north, the kitchen. In its prime, Tōfuku-ji was home to hundreds of persons, and so the kitchen had to be a gigantic facility to prepare sufficient food, even though in their Zen simplicity meals consisted almost exclusively of rice, rice gruel, soup, and pickled vegetables. The kitchen building also housed the monastery's administrative offices. The two buildings situated on the central axis inside the mountain gate, the Buddha Hall and the Dharma Hall from south to north, round out the seven essential buildings of the Sung model. The Buddha Hall, with its often-lavish statuary and other artwork, was the site of many of the monastery's formal ceremonies. The Dharma Hall might be thought of as the teaching hall. However, teaching consisted not in giving and receiving formal lectures, but rather was a forum for discussion between the abbot and the other members of the community.

One of the chief primary sources of information about the layout of classical Zen monasteries is a painting of Tōfuku-ji by the great medieval artist Sesshū Tōyō (1420–1506). This painting, which currently resides at Tōfuku-ji, clearly shows the seven main buildings, or their predecessors, as described above, framed by the eastern mountains in the background. Four of Tōfuku-ji's medieval buildings, the monks' hall (constructed around 1340), the mountain gate, the latrine, and the bathhouse, have survived to the present. They are classified as National Treasures or Important Cultural Properties, and remain among the best and oldest examples of medieval monastic architecture in Japan. The latrine is probably the only outhouse anywhere that is recognized as one of its country's greatest cultural artifacts! These buildings owe their survival at least in part to Tōfuku-ji's location on the southeast fringe of Kyoto, where it was relatively removed from the battles that devastated Kyoto, particularly during the Ōnin War (1467–1477).

Although Tōfuku-ji's founding and early sponsorship are credited to the courtier Michiie, it like all of the *gozan* monasteries depended heavily on the financial support and

The Main Hall, Tōfuku-ji Monastery.

The Kaisando Hall (Jōrakuan Hermitage), Tōfuku-ji Monastery.

political protection of the shogunate. Tōfuku-ji's ties with Japan's military and political leadership continued from the medieval era to early modern times. The first of the three great unifiers of modern Japan, Oda Nobunaga (1534–1582), established his headquarters at Tōfuku-ji when he marched to Kyoto in 1568 to establish his military and political hegemony in the capital. The last of the unifiers, Tokugawa Ieyasu (1542–1616), chose Tōfuku-ji as the burial site of his wife, who was also the sister of the second unifier, Toyotomi Hideyoshi (1536–1598).

The Buddhist establishment, and the *gozan* monasteries in particular, included as members a very large proportion of the Japanese that were familiar with China and able to communicate with Chinese in their own language. China remained Japan's chief trading partner and source of cultural ideas during medieval times, even during and following the relatively brief incursion by European merchants and missionaries in the latter half of the sixteenth and early part of the seventeenth centuries. That being the case, Zen monks were in great demand as members of trading missions and as arbiters on cultural matters. Although land income and donations from wealthy patrons constituted the chief fiscal support of most monasteries, many profited significantly from their involvement with mercantile ventures to China, and some even organized their own trading missions.

It is almost impossible to exaggerate the importance of the Zen sect and that of individual monks in the development of Japanese culture. The same Eisai who introduced Zen into Japan also brought tea, and especially the cultivation of tea, from China. Perhaps initially used as a stimulant to aid monks during their long hours of meditation, tea early on assumed a ritualistic significance in Zen life that is akin to, and goes beyond, that of wine in the Christian Eucharist. Tea drinking was subsequently adopted by the general population, starting with the warrior class, and developed into one of the greatest and most characteristically Japanese of Japanese art forms, the tea ceremony.

Japanese calligraphy has Chinese roots that are much older than Japanese Zen, but calligraphy came to be closely associated with Zen and Zen monks as the acceptance of Zen increased. Sayings and instruction were rendered in exquisite calligraphy and placed in monasteries for the guidance of resident monks. The general population also valued these calligraphic works as sources of edification, as well as on purely aesthetic grounds. Zen practitioners were among the artists who produced calligraphy that not only can enhance the meaning of the words being rendered, but also can arouse aesthetic appreciation beyond, and even independent of, that meaning.

Closely associated with calligraphy is the art of monochrome ink painting, and here again Zen adherents were pushing the artistic frontiers. Zen legends provided the subjects for many ink paintings that were executed for the edification or the aesthetic enjoyment of the viewer. Furthermore, the austerity of Zen and the non-explicit nature of its teachings profoundly influenced the stark simplicity of ink painting, wherein a few brush strokes merely suggest rather than realistically depict the subject. Very frequently calligraphy and painting, typically by different artists, were combined in the same piece, the calligraphy serving to elucidate the painting at the same time that the painting illustrates the calligraphy, both working together harmoniously. Finally, as might be expected, Zen monks were the primary carriers of the latest techniques in ink painting from China to Japan.

Nō, the great traditional theater of Japan, like calligraphy, has roots that predate Japanese Zen. Nonetheless, Zen profoundly influenced Nō, providing some of the important classical themes for Nō plays, such as the transient nature of existence and the pain that is caused by clinging to things. Like ink painting, Nō received from Zen much of its reliance on techniques that merely suggest rather than realistically portray dramatic happenings. It has even been postulated that the slow, deliberate dance by which the Nō actor makes his way along the passageway to the stage, evoking what the great Nō theoretician and playwright Motokiyo Zeami (1363–1443) termed *yūgen* or "underlying mystery," was shaped by the monastery hallway through which the monk trainee with a profound sense of awe approached his Zen Master for daily private interviews.

Arts from flower arranging and poetry, especially haiku, to swordsmanship and archery bear the distinctive mark of Zen thought and practice. Zen monks were among the leading practitioners and teachers of each of these characteristically Japanese art forms, and Zen thought provided much of their philosophical underpinning. In each case, the contributions of Zen include the value of simplicity, austerity, and suggestion; a sense of the inadequacy of the verbal, the explicit, and the intellectual; the illusory nature of the commonly perceived dualities of good and evil, life and death, self and other; the importance of avoiding attachments that cause one to cling to things; reliance on one's self, as opposed to an external benevolent or even divine being, as the agent of one's own enlightenment or inspiration; and the supreme self-discipline, as well as techniques for its attainment, that are required in the pursuit of enlightenment or inspiration.

From its inception, Tōfuku-ji and members of its community fostered and valued these art forms, but none so much as calligraphy and ink painting. The foremost medieval artist, Sesshū, was sufficiently attracted to and inspired by Tōfuku-ji to have painted its definitive depiction cited above—arguably the most definitive depiction of any medieval Japanese monastery. Tōfuku-ji still houses some masterpieces painted by Sesshū, as well as copies of Sesshū's work. The monk Kitsuzan Minchō (1352–1431) established an active painting tradition at Tōfuku-ji. A noted member of his line was the Tōfuku-ji monk Reisai, who was active in Kyoto from around 1435 to the late 1460s. The important Momoyama-era painter Kaihō Yūshō (1533–1615) as a youngster enrolled as a novice monk at Tōfuku-ji, where he remained as a lay priest. Apparently the abbot was sufficiently impressed with his talent that he arranged for him to study with one of the leading artists of the time, Kanō Motonobu (1476–1559). One of Motonobu's descendents, Kanō Eitoku (1543–1590), was commissioned in

Tsūten bridge is famous for its view of autumn leaves, especially the Chinese and Japanese maples.

1588 to cover the ceiling of Tōfuku-ji's Dharma Hall with a monochrome painting of a dragon. Eitoku was in failing health at the time, so the commission was completed in turn by his adopted son, Kanō Sanraku (1559–1635). The enormous dragon is still visible today, glowering down majestically from the heavens. In Zen art, dragons customarily are symbolic of great spiritual energy.

The medieval era without question was the time when Zen monasteries were at their greatest and most influential. During the Tokugawa era (1600–1868), Zen along with Japanese Buddhism in general went through a gradual decline, yielding intellectual and philosophical leadership to Confucianism. This was especially true of the *gozan* monasteries. Indeed, none of the current branches of Rinzai Zen derive from any of the *gozan* monasteries. Instead, modern Rinzai has the Myōshin-ji Monastery as its ancestor, through the great Tokugawa era monk Hakuin Zenji (1686–1769), who almost single-handedly revived Japanese Zen. During the early part of the Meiji period (1868–1912), Buddhism was actually persecuted in favor of the indigenous Shinto religion, as one facet of early Meiji efforts to restore ancient, uniquely

Japanese customs and ways of doing things, including an emperor with the power to rule the country. The persecution was soon lifted and replaced by religious tolerance, but much damage had been done, and only with supreme effort could Zen monasteries recover even a shadow of their former brilliance.

When Fukushima Keidō was appointed Head Abbot of Tōfuku-ji in 1980, its training hall had no monks and only a few cats. After just seven years under his leadership, it had grown to twenty-five monks, and Tōfuku-ji remains a viable training institution for Zen priests. Today's monks are subject to much the same rigorous discipline that their early forebears inherited from Sung China. The daily schedule typically includes seven hours of *zazen* (seated meditation)—much more than that during the special intensive training sessions that occur several times each year. It also includes several hours of manual labor, mendication, individual discussions with the abbot, sutra chanting, highly ritualized meals, and prescribed attention to personal hygiene. In the few hours that remain, the monks are able to sleep and rest. After approximately three years of monastery training, a monk typically leaves Tōfuku-ji for assignment as a priest in his own temple. Tōfuku-ji heads a complex of twenty-three subtemples in Kyoto, as well as 370 subsidiary temples of the Tōfuku-ji sect throughout Japan.

Tōfuku-ji remains an important center for Zen art. In addition to its magnificent buildings and gardens, it is the home of hundreds of masterpieces of painting and calligraphy, many of which date to medieval times. Abbot Fukushima himself continues the tradition of the Zen calligrapher. He typically sets aside five or ten days each month from his monastery duties to concentrate on doing calligraphy, and his work has been published in numerous books and articles. His annual American tours of universities and museums include demonstrations of calligraphy, which are extremely well received.

Appendix

SHORT BIOGRAPHIES OF THREE ZEN MASTERS

Shibayama Zenkei Rōshi

1894: Born in Aichi Prefecture, Japan.

1904: Ordained as Zen monk of the Rinzai sect at Kokubun-ji (Aichi Prefecture).

1947: Becomes the Zen Master (Rōshi) of Nanzen-ji Monastery in Kyoto.

1959: Becomes the Head Abbot of the Nazen-ji branch of the Rinzai sect.

1965–1973: Annual visits to universities in the United States to lecture on Zen.

1974: Dies. *Zen Comments on the Mumonkan* is published.

Okada Kido Rōshi

1902: Born in Hiroshima Prefecture.

1913: Ordained as a Zen monk of the Rinzai sect at Høfuku-ji in Okayama Prefecture.

1950: Becomes Zen Master (Rōshi) of Hōfuku-ji Monastery.

1981: Becomes Head Abbot of the Tōfuku-ji Branch of the Rinzai sect.

1988: Dies.

Fukushima Keidō Rōshi

March 1933: Born in the city of Kobe, Japan.

May 1947: Ordained as a Zen monk of the Rinzai sect by Okada Kido Rōshi (Head Abbot of the Tōfuku-ji Branch of the Rinzai sect).

March 1961: Graduated from Ōtani University (in Kyoto) with a doctorate in Chinese Buddhism.

April 1961–February 1972: Trains as a Zen monk at Nanzen-ji Monastery (in Kyoto) under Shibayama Zenkei Rōshi, Head Abbot of the Nanzen-ji Branch of the Rinzai sect.

February–April, 1969: Visits Claremont College in California as the assistant to Shibayama Rōshi.

February 1973–February 1974: Works at the Institute of Religion and Culture at the Claremont graduate school, where he is a lecturer on Zen Buddhism and *zazen* practice.

October 1980–present: Zen Master (Rōshi) of Tōfuku-ji Monastery.

February 1989–present: Annual visitation to over twenty-five universities in the United States to lecture on Zen, to conduct *zazen*, and to perform calligraphy demonstrations.

April 1991–present: Head Abbot of the Tōfuku-ji Branch of the Rinzai sect.

LIST OF CONTRIBUTORS

Stephen Addiss is Tucker-Boatwright Professor at the University of Richmond. His art has been exhibited in Asia, Europe, and the United States, and he is the author of *The Art of Zen, Old Taoist,* and *How to Look at Japanese Art* (with Audrey Yoshiko Seo).

Ronald L. Carlisle received his undergraduate degree in religion and his doctorate in mathematics, both from Emory University. Since 1985 he has served as Professor of Computer Science and Mathematics at Oglethorpe University. In 1998 he participated in the AAC&U's Japan Seminar. In 1999 he enjoyed a brief residency at the Tōfuku-ji Monastery. He is one of Fukushima Keidō's American disciples.

Stephen J. Goldberg is Associate Professor of Asian Art History at Hamilton College. He has published extensively in the fields of Chinese calligraphy and painting. His research interests range from the history and aesthetics of Chinese calligraphy to cross-cultural comparative aesthetics. His forthcoming book is entitled *The Inscriptive Subject: Tradition and the Construction of Identity in Chinese Painting and Calligraphy* (State University of New York Press). He frequently conducts workshops on the teaching of Asian art, philosophy, and culture.

Lloyd Nick is the Director of the Oglethorpe University Museum of Art in Atlanta, Georgia, as well as a painter in his own right.

Audrey Yoshiko Seo, Ph.D., is an independent scholar of Japanese art who specializes in Zen painting and calligraphy of the 17th through 20th centuries. She is the principal author of *The Art of Twentieth-Century Zen: Paintings and Calligraphy by Japanese Masters.*

Jeff Shore is Professor of International Zen at Hanazono University in Kyoto. He has studied and practiced Zen for over thirty years, the last twenty at the Tōfuku-ji Monastery with Fukushima Rōshi. He was born in 1953 in the Philadelphia area and is also a writer, translator, and lecturer for Zen retreats in Europe and North America.

Jason Wirth is Associate Professor of Philosophy at Oglethorpe University, concentrating in the areas of Continental Philosophy, Comparative Philosophy (Philosophy East and West), and Aesthetics. His new book is *The Conspiracy of Life: Meditations on Schelling and His Time* (State University of New York Press). He is also the curator of Asian Art for the Oglethorpe University Museum of Art.

LIST OF PLATES

Plate 1, page 14

Fukushima Keidō (1933–), *Mu*

ink on paper, 13.5" x 53".

無

Plate 2, page 19

Fukushima Keidō, *Hey, Throw it Away*

Ink on paper, 13.5" x 53."

咄　放下著

Plate 3, page 23

Fukushima Keidō, *Barrier*

Ink on paper, 13.5" x 53".

関

Plate 4, page 25

Fukushima Keidō, *Mushin*

Ink on paper, 13.5" x 53".

無心

Plate 5, page 27

Fukushima Keidō, *Pure and Empty*

Ink on paper, 13.5" x 53".

清虚

Plate 6, page 30

Fukushima Keidō, *Bright and Clear*

Ink on paper, 13.5" x 53".

明歴々

Plate 7, page 33

Fukushima Keidō, *Appear with Dignity*

Ink on paper, 13.5" x 53".

露度々

Plate 8, page 35

Fukushima Keidō, *Everywhere and Everytime Become a Master*

Ink on paper, 13.5" x 53".

隨處作主

Plate 9, page 37

Fukushima Keidō, *Vast Emptiness, Nothing Sacred*

Ink on paper, 13.5" x 53".

廓然無聖

Plate 10, page 39

Fukushima Keidō, *I Don't Know*

Ink on paper, 13.5" x 53".

不職

Plate 11, page 41

Fukushima Keidō, *Go Have Some Tea*

Ink on paper, 13.5" x 53".

喫茶去

Plate 12, page 45

Fukushima Keidō, *Every Day Is a Good Day*

Ink on paper, 13.5" x 53".

日々是好日

Plate 19, page 83

Fukushima Keidō, *Ensō: No Guest or Host*

Ink on paper, 13.5" x 53".

円相無賓主

Plate 20, page 87

Fukushima Keidō, *Ensō: Watch, Touch and Bite*

Ink on paper, 13.5" x 53".

Plate 21, page 89

Attributed to Sesshū Tōyō (1420–1506), *Bodhidharma*

Ink on paper, 33" x 75.75".

Plate 22, page 93

Shibayama Zenkei (1894–1974)and D. T. Suzuki (1869–1966),

Wondrous [right side, done by Suzuki]

and *Making Fire in Water* [left side, done by Shibayama]

Ink on paper, 19.5" x 11.25".

妙　火向水中焚

Plate 23, page 97

Okada Rōshi, *Don't Have Wrong Thought*

Ink on paper, 16" x 14".

幕妄想

Plate 24, page 101

Shibayama Rōshi, *Nothing Is Everything, Everything Is Nothing*

Ink on paper, 12.75" x 52".

空即是色　色即是空

BIBLIOGRAPHY

(N.B., Japanese and Chinese names follow the custom of listing the family name first. When they are the primary authors, they are cited without a comma between the family name and the personal name.)

Addiss, Stephen. *The Art of Zen: Paintings and Calligraphy by Japanese Monks, 1600-1925.* New York: Harry N. Abrams, 1989.

Akamatsu Toshihide, and Philip B Yampolsky. "Muromachi Zen and the Gozan System," in *Japan in the Muromachi Age.* Edited by John W. Hall and Toyoda Takeshi. Berkeley: University of California Press, 1977.

Anesaki Masaharu. *History of Japanese Religion.* Rutland, Vermont and Tokyo: Tuttle, 1963.

Awakawa Yasuichi. *Zen Painting.* Translated by John Bester. New York and Tokyo: Kodansha International, 1970.

Bielefeldt, Carl. "Kokan Shiren and the Sectarian Uses of History," in *The Origins of Japan's Medieval World.* Edited by Jeffrey P. Mass. Stanford: Stanford University Press, 1997.

The Blue Cliff Record (Japanese: *Hekiganroku*). Translated by Thomas Cleary and J. C. Cleary. Boston: Shambhala Publications, 1977.

Brinker, Helmut, and Kanazawa Hiroshi. *Zen Masters of Meditation in Images and Writings.* Zurich: Artibus Asiae Publishers, Supplementum 40, 1996.

Bush, Susan. *The Chinese Literati on Painting from Su Shih (1037–1101) to Tung Ch'i-ch'ang (1555–1636),* Harvard-Yenching Institute Studies 27, 2nd ed. Cambridge, Mass: Harvard University Press, 1978.

Chuang Tzu. *Chuang Tzu: Basic Writings.* Translated by Burton Watson. New York: Columbia University Press, 1964.

Collcutt, Martin. *Five Mountains: The Rinzai Zen Monastic Institution in Medieval Japan.* Cambridge: Harvard University Press, 1981.

_____. "Zen and the Gozan," in *The Cambridge History of Japan,* Volume 3, *Medieval Japan.* Edited by Yamamura Kozo. Cambridge: Cambridge University Press, 1990.

Fielding, Helen. "Envisioning the Other: Lacan and Merleau-Ponty on Intersubjectivity," in *Merleau-Ponty, Intersubjectivity and Exteriority, Physical Life and the World.* Edited by Dorothea Olkowski and James Morely. Albany: State University of New York Press, 1999.

Fu Shen C. Y. "Huang T'ing-chien's Calligraphy and His *Scroll for Chang Ta-t'ung:* A Masterpiece Written in Exile," Ph.D. diss., Princeton University, 1976

Goldberg, Stephen J. "Tradition and Authorial Identity in Chinese Calligraphy: Three Works from the Elliott Collection," in *Oriental Art*, Vol. XLVVI, no. 5 (2000).

Hakuin. *Wild Ivy: The Spiritual Autobiography of Zen Master Hakuin.* Translated by Norman Waddell. Boston: Shambhala, 1999.

———. *Zen Master Hakuin: Selected Writings.* Translated by Philip B. Yampolsky. New York: Columbia University Press, 1971.

Harrist, Robert E. Jr., and Wen C. Fong. *The Embodied Image: Chinese Calligraphy from the John B. Elliott Collection.* Princeton: The Art Museum, Princeton University, in association with Harry N. Abrams, Inc., 1999.

Hickman, Money L., ed. *Japan's Golden Age: Momoyama.* New Haven: Yale University Press, 1996.

Hisamatsu Shin'ichi. *Formless Self Awakening.* Edited by Jeff Shore. Unpublished manuscript.

———. *Zen and the Fine Arts.* Translated by Tokiwa Gishin. New York and Tokyo: Kodansha International, 1971.

Huang, Martin W. *Desire and Fictional Narrative in Late Imperial China.* Cambridge, Mass.: Harvard University Asia Center, 2001.

Jōshū. *The Recorded Sayings of Zen Master Jōshū.* Translated by James Green. Boston: Shambhala Publications, 1998.

Kasulis, Tom. *Zen Action, Zen Person.* Honolulu: University of Hawai'i Press, 1985.

Keane, Webb. *Signs of Recognition: Powers and Hazards of Representation in an Indonesian Society.* Berkeley: University of California Press, 1997.

Kitagawa, Joseph M. *Religion in Japanese History.* New York: Columbia University Press, 1966.

Klee, Felix. *Paul Klee.* Translated by Richard and Clara Winston. New York: Georges Braziller, 1962.

Lafleur, William R. "Saigyō and the Buddhist Value of Nature," in *Nature in Asian Traditions of Thought: Essays in Environmental Philosophy.* Edited by J. Baird Callicott and Roger T. Ames. Albany: State University of New York Press, 1989.

Ledderose, Lothar. *Mi Fu and the Classical Tradition of Chinese Calligraphy.* Princeton: Princeton University Press, 1979.

Merleau-Ponty, Maurice. *Signs.* Translated by Richard C. McCleary. Evanston: Northwestern University Press, 1964.

Munsterberg, Hugo. *Zen and Oriental Art.* Rutland, Vermont and Tokyo: Charles Tuttle, 1965.

Nakata Yujirō. *The Art of Japanese Calligraphy.* Translated by A. Woodhull. New York and Tokyo: Weatherhill/Heibonsha, 1973.

Nakata Yujirō, editor. *A History of Art in China: Chinese Calligraphy.* Translated by Jeffrey Hunter. New York, Tokyo, Kyoto: Weatherhill/Tankosha, 1983.

Nietzsche, Friedrich. *Ecce Homo* (1888). Translated by R. J. Hollingdale. New York and London: Penguin, 1979.

_____. *Twilight of the Idols* (1888). Translated by R. J. Hollingdale. New York and London: Penguin, 1990.

_____. *Werke in drei Bänden.* Edited by Karl Schlechta. Munich: Carl Hansler Verlag, 1955.

Nishida Kitarō. *Art and Morality* (1923). Translated by David Dilworth and Valdo Viglielmo. Honolulu: University of Hawai'i Press, 1973.

Nishimura Eshin. *Unsui: A Diary of Zen Monastic Life.* Edited by Bardwell Smith. Honolulu: University of Hawai'i Press, 1993.

Nishitani Keiji. *Religion and Nothingness.* Translated by Jan van Bragt. Berkeley: University of California Press, 1982.

_____. *The Self-Overcoming of Nihilism.* Translated by Graham Parkes and Aihara Setsuko. Albany: State University of New York Press, 1990.

Rosenfield, John M. "The Unity of the Three Creeds: A Theme in Japanese Ink Painting of the Fifteenth Century," in *Japan in the Muromachi Age.* Edited by John W. Hall and Toyoda Takeshi. Berkeley: University of California Press, 1977.

Ōmori Sōgen and Terayama Katsujō. *Zen and the Art of Calligraphy: The Essence of Sho.* Translated by John Stevens. London: Arkana, 1983.

Sadler, A. L. *The Maker of Modern Japan: The Life of Tokugawa Ieyasu.* New York: AMS Press, 1977.

Seo, Audrey Yoshiko, and Addiss, Stephen. *The Art of Twentieth-Century Zen: Paintings and Calligraphy by Japanese Masters.* Boston: Shambhala, 1998.

Shibayama Zenkei. *A Flower Does Not Talk.* Rutland, Vermont and Tokyo: Charles Tuttle, 1970.

_____. *Zen Comments on the Mumonkan.* Translated by Kudo Sumiko. New York: Harper & Row, 1974.

Sōetsu Yanagi. *The Unknown Craftsman: A Japanese Insight into Beauty*. New York and Tokyo: Kodansha International, revised edition, 1989.

Stevens, John. *Sacred Calligraphy of the East*. Boulder and London: Shambhala, 1981.

Sturman, Peter. *Mi Fu: Style and the Art of Calligraphy in Northern Song China*. New Haven and London: Yale University Press, 1997.

Sun Qianli. "Treatise on Calligraphy," in *Two Chinese Treatises on Calligraphy*. Translated by Chang Ch'ung-ho and Hans H. Frankel. New Haven and London: Yale University Press, 1995

Suzuki Daisetz Teitaro. *Zen and Japanese Culture*. New York: Pantheon, 1959.

Suzuki Shunryū. *Zen Mind, Beginner's Mind*. Edited by Trudy Dixon. New York and Tokyo: Weatherhill, 1970.

Tiedemann, Arthur E., ed. *An Introduction to Japanese Civilization*. New York: Columbia University Press, 1974.

Trungpa, Chögyam. *The Art of Calligraphy: Joining Heaven and Earth*. Edited by Judith L. Lief. Boston and London: Shambhala, 1994.

Varley, Paul. *Japanese Culture*. New York: Praeger, 1973.

INDEX